POWER-CARVING

a Chesapeake Bay BLUE CRAB

ALAN (MICKEY) BROWN

Schiffer Publishing Ltd
4880 Lower Valley Road Atglen, Pennsylvania 19310

Library of Congress Control Number: 2011943816

Designed by Justin Watkinson Cover By Bruce Waters
Type set in CityD/NewBskvll BT

ISBN: 978-0-7643-3965-3
Printed in China

Published by Schiffer Publishing Ltd.
4880 Lower Valley Road
Atglen, PA 19310
Phone: (610) 593-1777; Fax: (610) 593-2002
E-mail: Info@schifferbooks.com

In Europe, Schiffer books are distributed by
Bushwood Books
6 Marksbury Ave.
Kew Gardens
Surrey TW9 4JF England
Phone: 44 (0) 20 8392 8585; Fax: 44 (0) 20 8392 9876
E-mail: info@bushwoodbooks.co.uk
Website: www.bushwoodbooks.co.uk

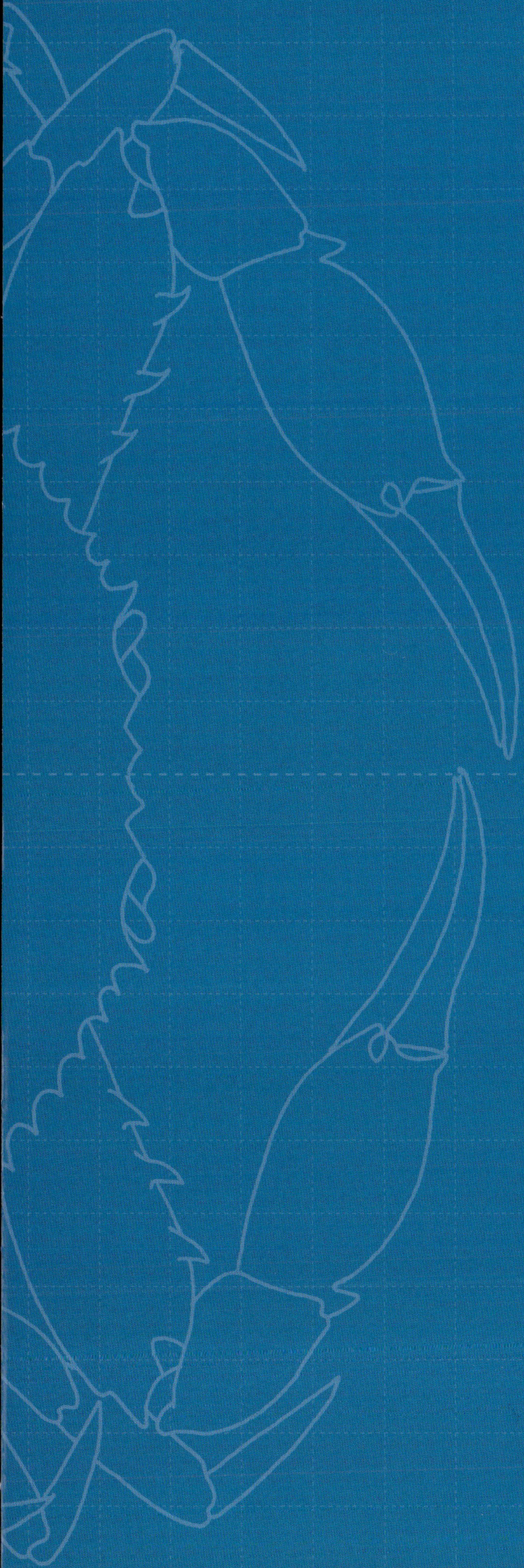

DEDICATION

To my older brother Bim, who encouraged and taught me the art of woodcarving. In my early years he was my life role model and opened many doors that helped guide me in my adult life. Bim helped me reach so many goals that would have been impossible without his help. He continues to be my role model and best friend.

SPECIAL THANKS

A very special thanks to my wife of fifty-eight years, Pat. Not only did she help with my neglected chores while I worked on this book, but she also took all of the photographs featured here.

I also want to thank my daughter-in-law Regina Brown for typing all of the text and captions. Not only is she a wonderful daughter-in-law, but also a very skilled typist.

CONTENTS

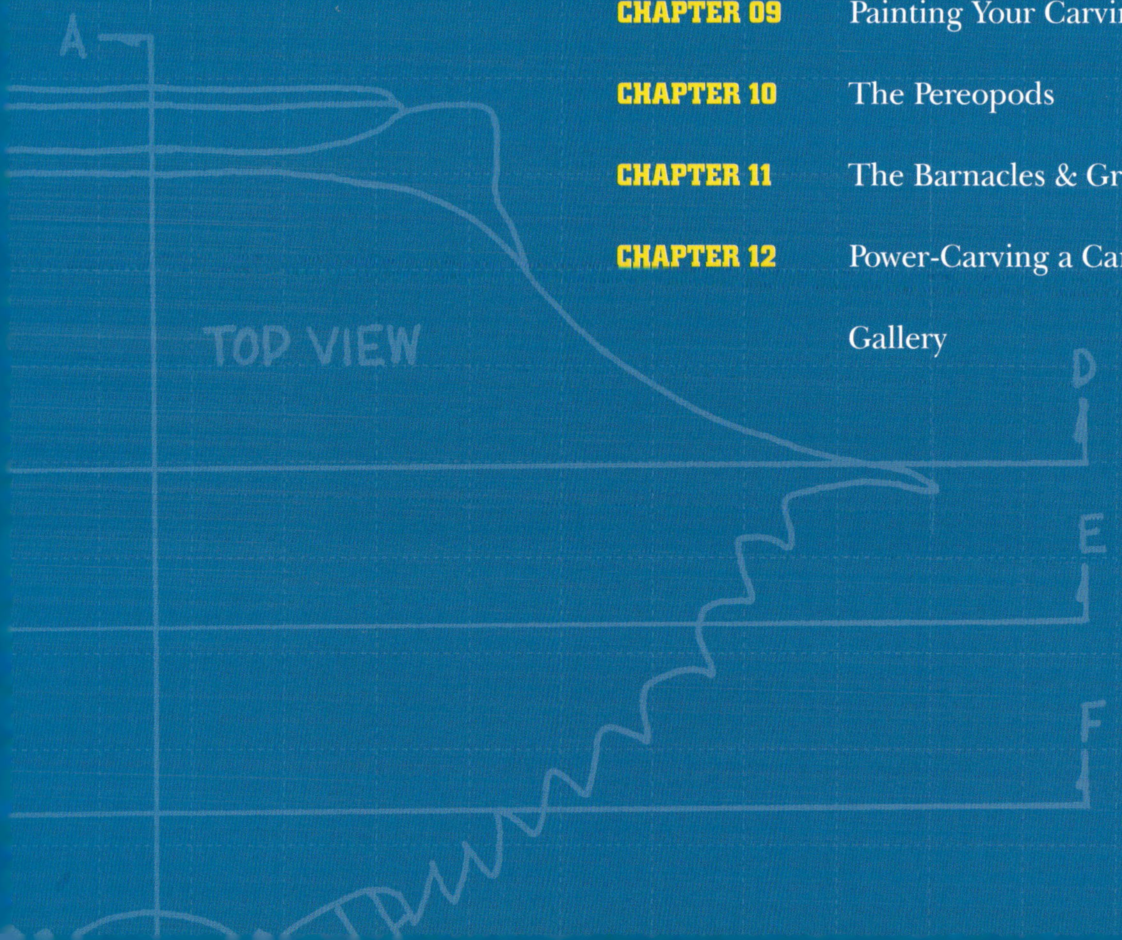

INTRODUCTION

This book will provide you, the carver, with a very detailed, full-scale set of drawings and numerous full-scale cross-sectional templates to insure a very accurate carving. It is my intent that through these full-scale drawings, cross-sectionals, and photographs you will know precisely the shape of every part of the blue crab and will not have to assume how it is to be carved.

Every step of the carving process is described with text and pictures to insure your complete success. While the beginning carver will surely enjoy the facets of this carving, the advanced woodcarver will find this crustacean project to be both challenging and rewarding. Color photographs are included here to assist you in true color identification.

I have also provided my own painting and coloring techniques. While I have attempted to paint the crab with acrylics, a brush, and minimum experience, I feel that an experienced airbrush painter would end up with a more realistic and attractive piece of art. Additional information will assist you in designing and constructing a nautical display background and base for the completed project.

From start to finish, you will learn much about the life cycle, nomenclature, and characteristics of this beautiful swimmer and crustacean, the Chesapeake Bay blue crab (Callinectes sapidus). I hope you will come to appreciate it as much as I do and take much pleasure in your carvings.

01 | BLUE CRAB ANATOMY & NOMENCLATURE

The Blue Crab exterior anatomy is labeled here so that you, the carver, can identify and become familiar with the correct names of the many parts of the crab to be carved.

Actual crab photographs are shown in each of the following chapters, describing the color and techniques necessary to paint each specific crab part. Hopefully, using the various views, will help you to realistically paint the carved blue crab.

The source used for identifying all the crab parts has been taken from the Blue Crab Archives (http://www.bluecrab.info/anatomy.html).

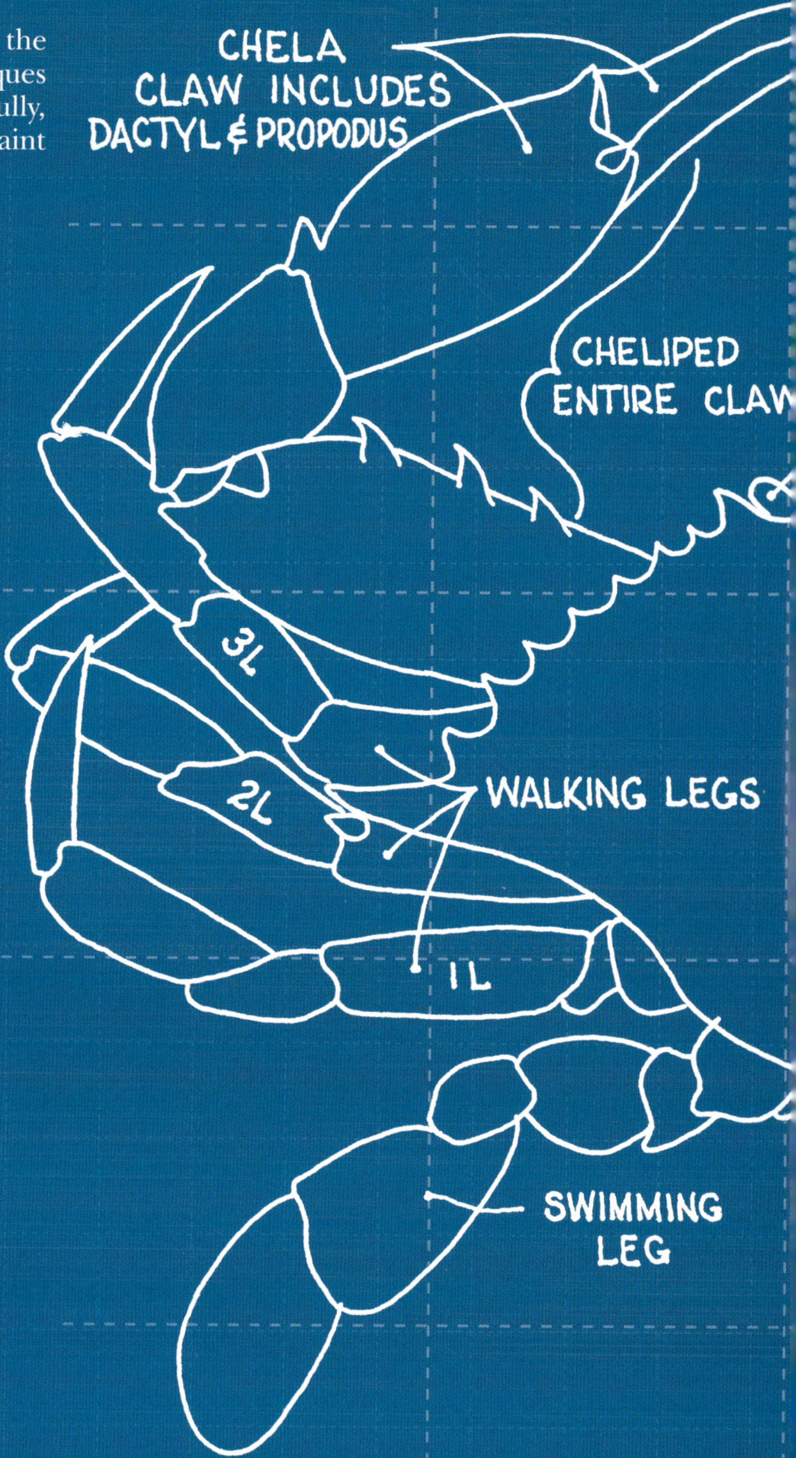

DRAWINGS & TEMPLATES

02

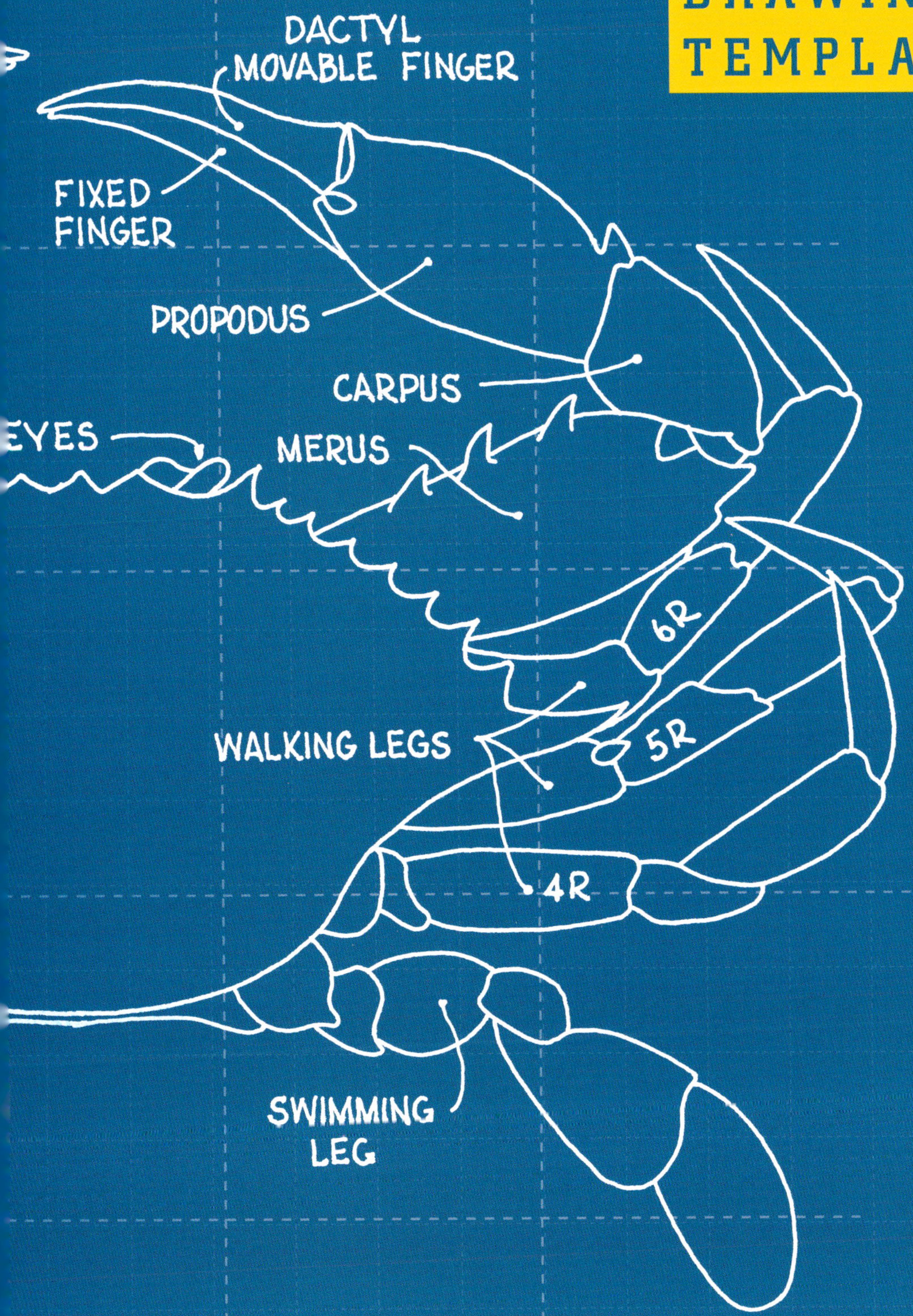

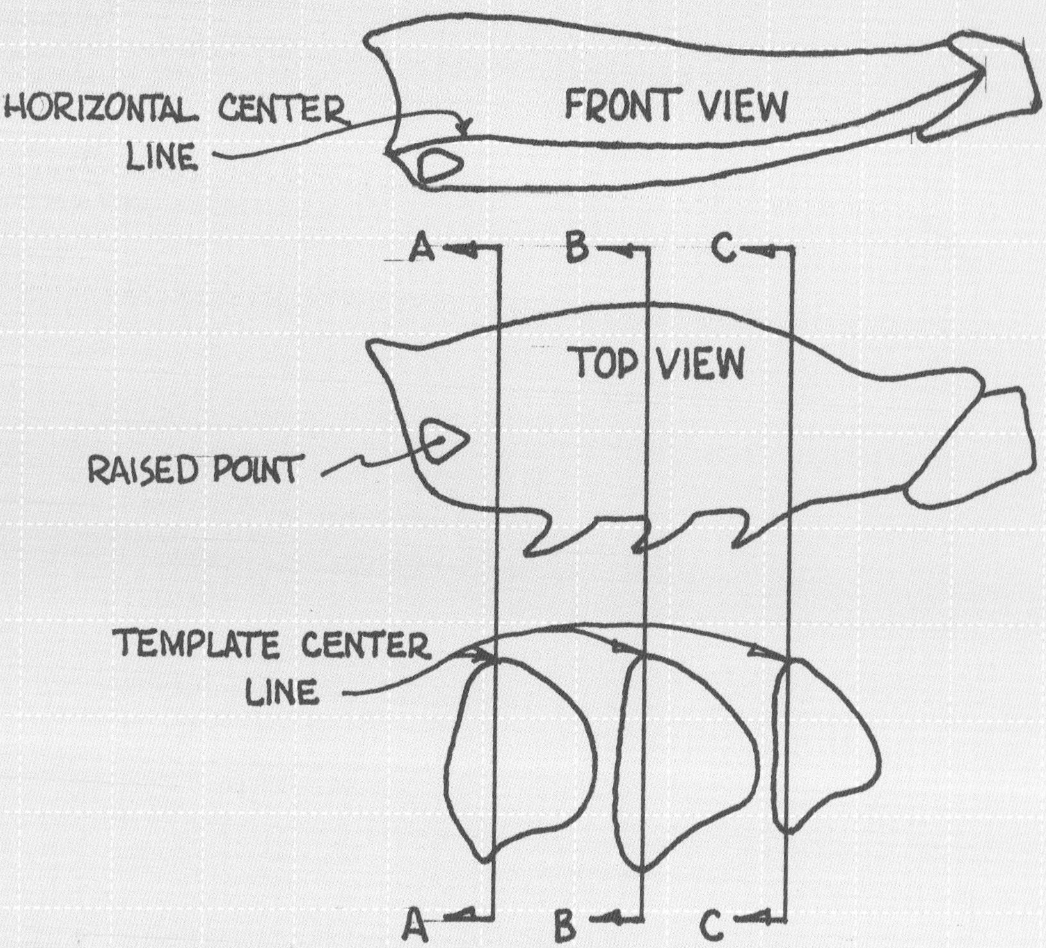

RIGHT MERUS

BARNACLE

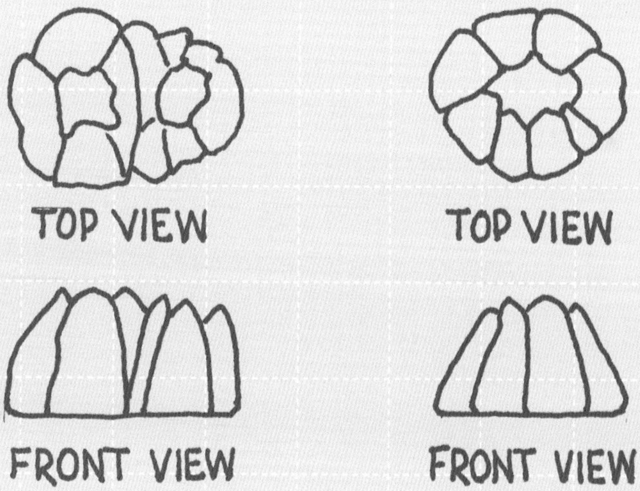

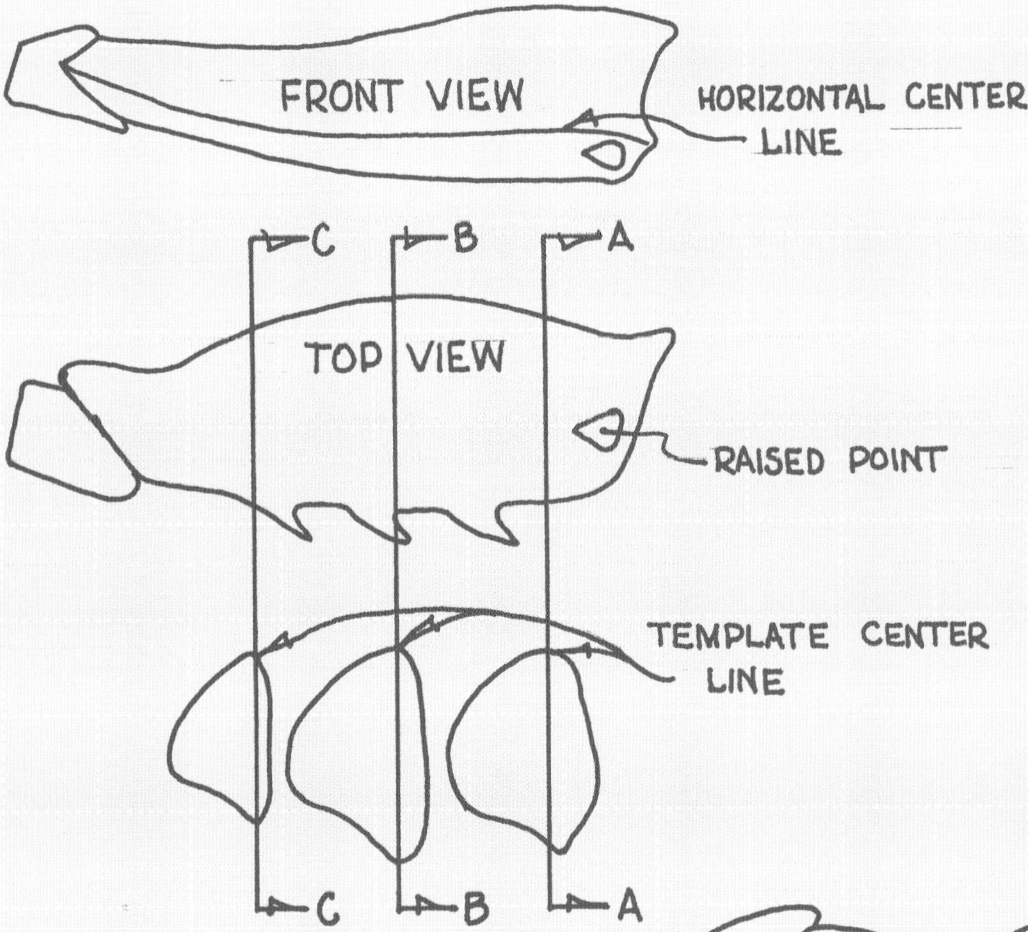

LEFT MERUS

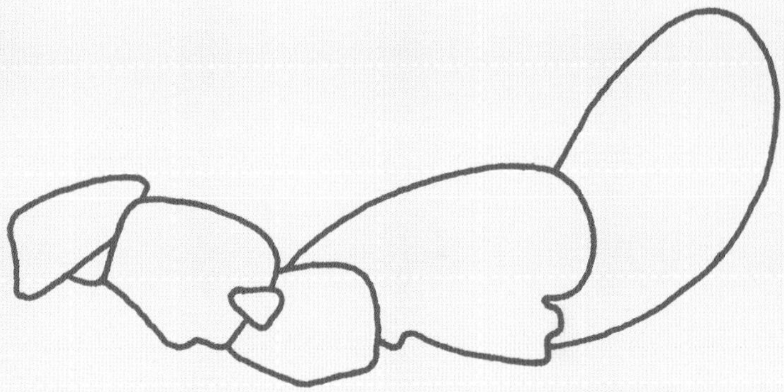

TOP VIEW LEFT SWIMMING LEG

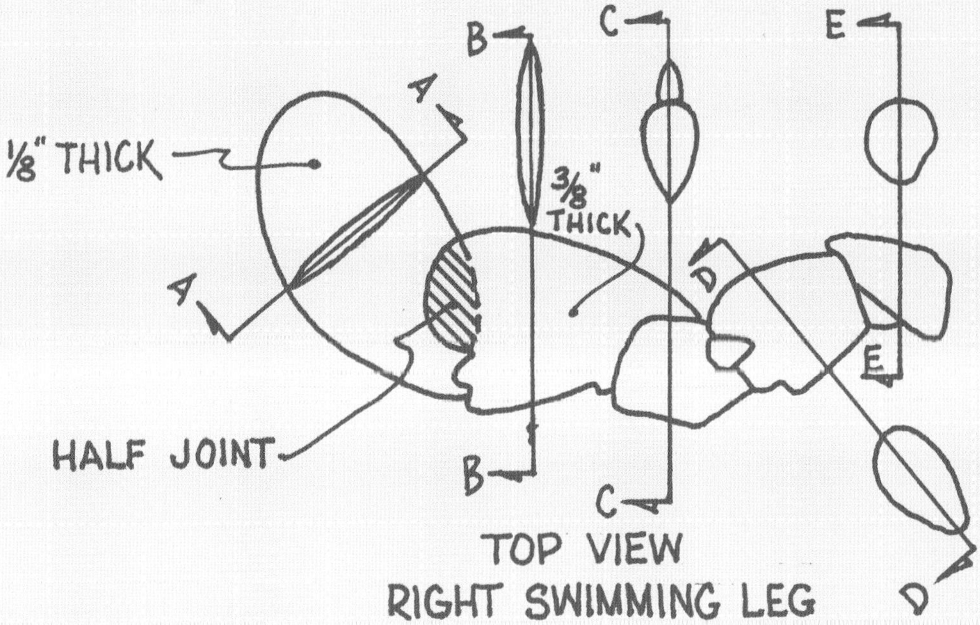

TOP VIEW
RIGHT SWIMMING LEG

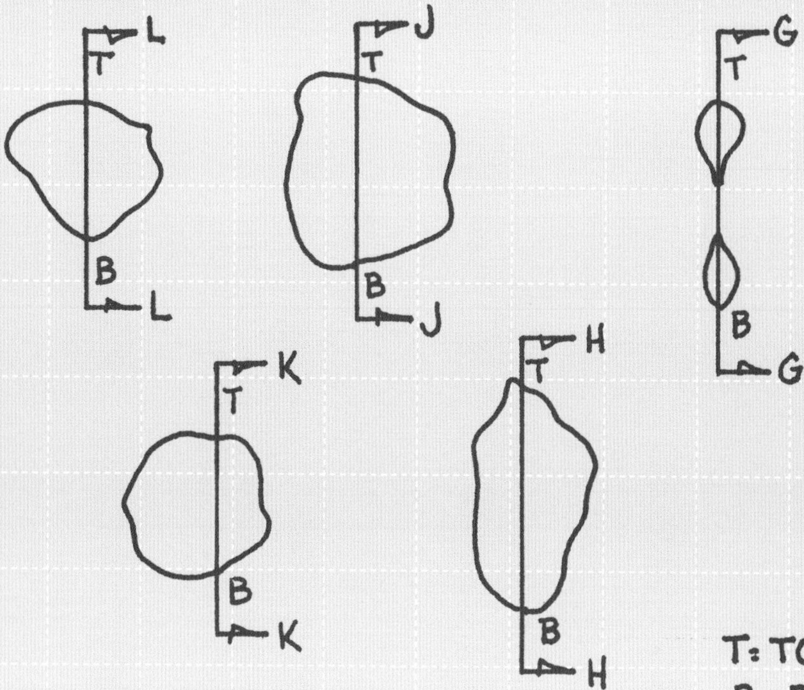

T: TOP
B = BOTTOM

LEFT CHELA - CARPUS

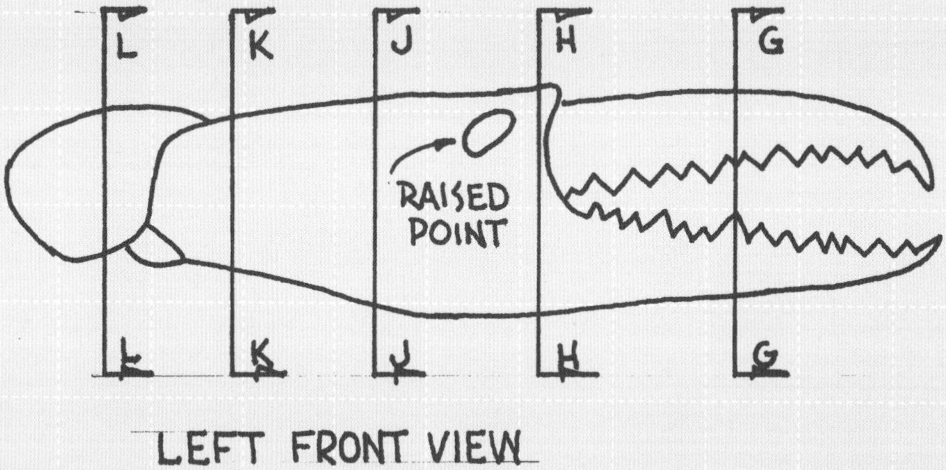

LEFT FRONT VIEW

LEFT TOP VIEW

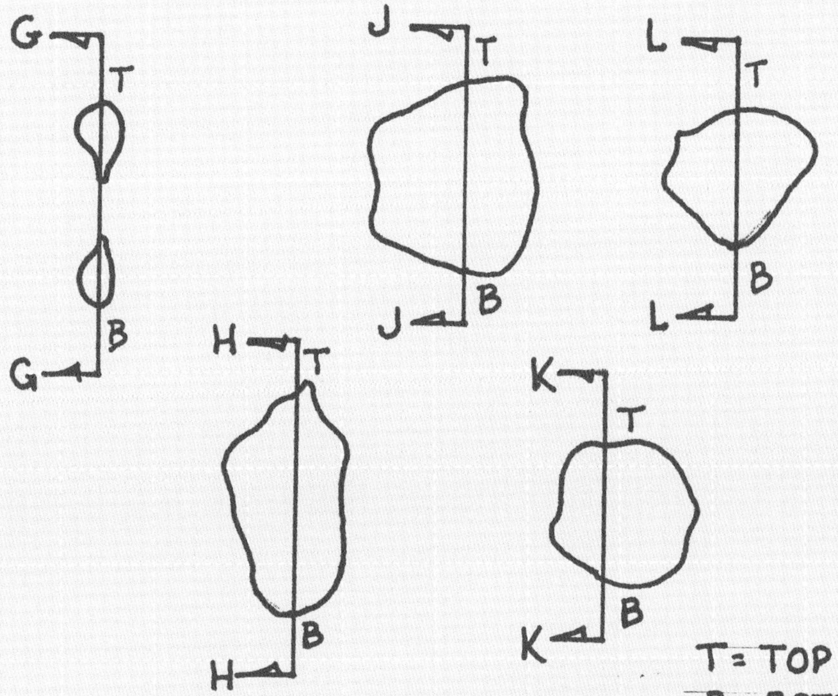

T = TOP
B = BOTTOM

RIGHT CHELA - CARPUS

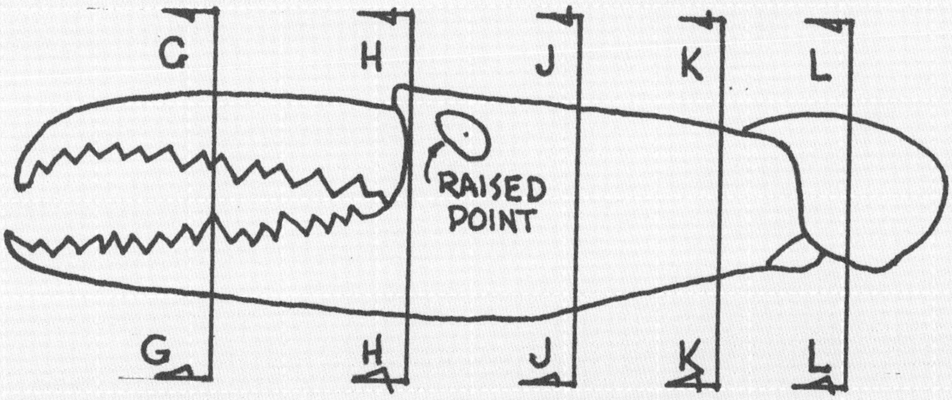

RIGHT FRONT VIEW

RIGHT TOP VIEW

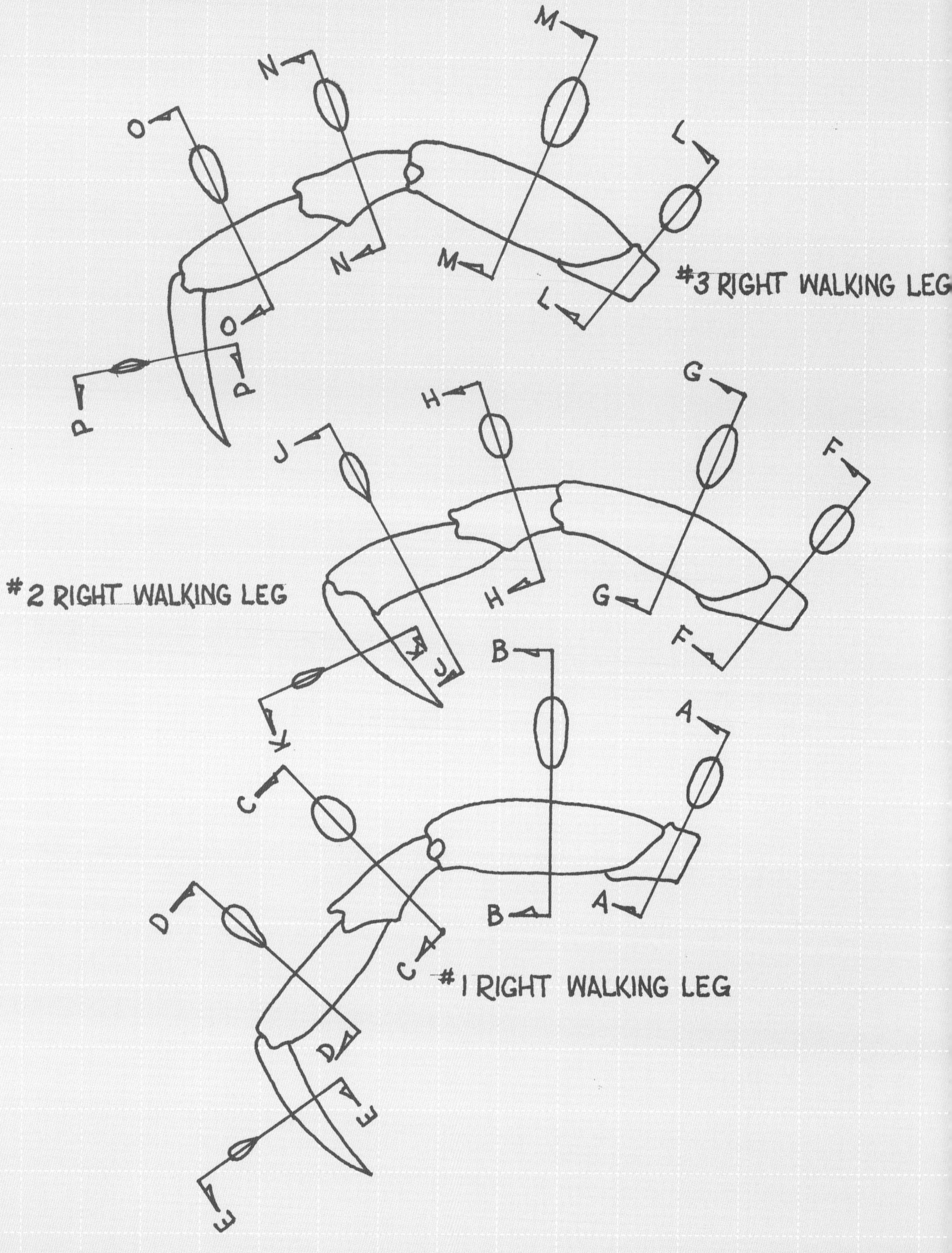
#3 RIGHT WALKING LEG
#2 RIGHT WALKING LEG
#1 RIGHT WALKING LEG

#6 LEFT WALKING LEG

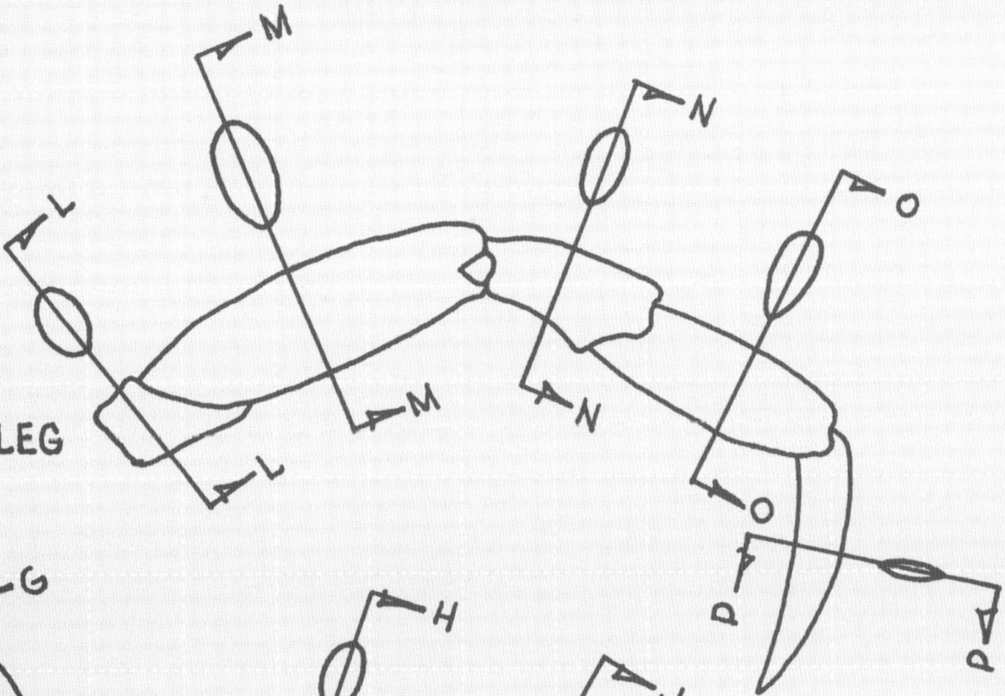

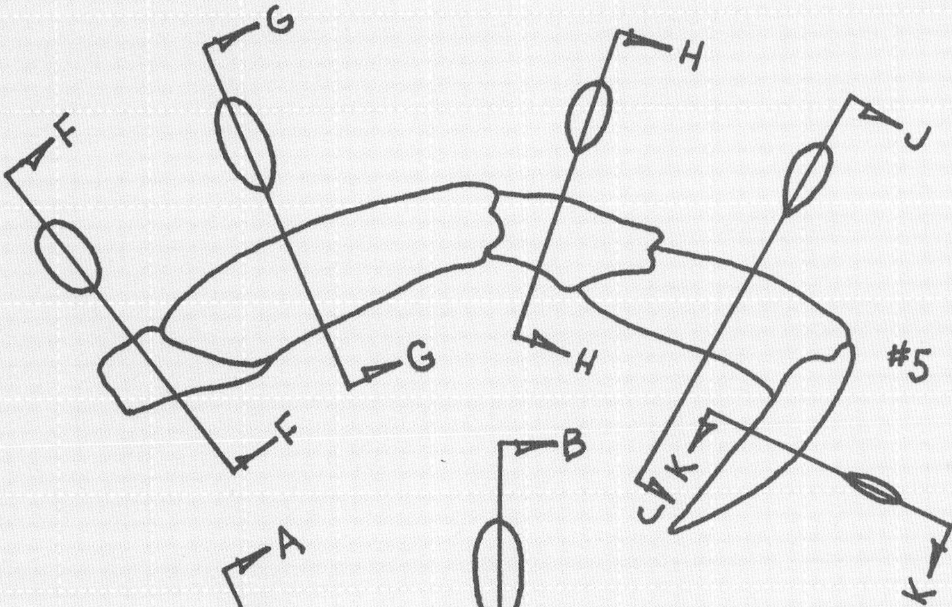

#5 LEFT WALKING LEG

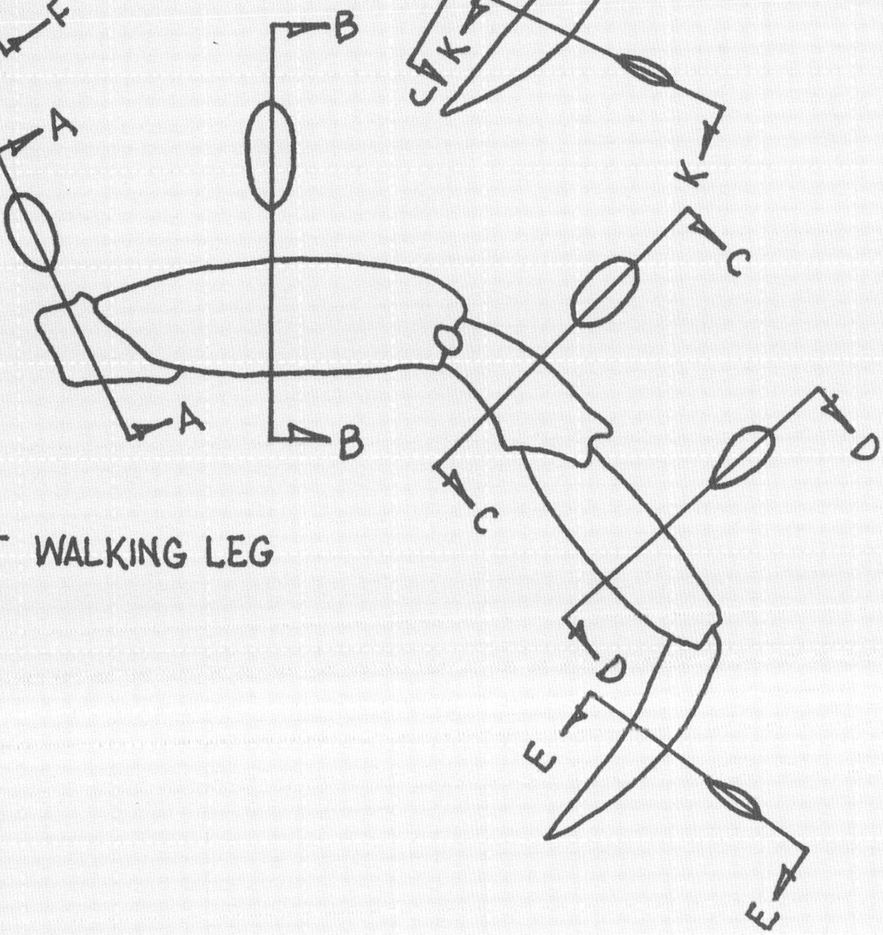

#4 LEFT WALKING LEG

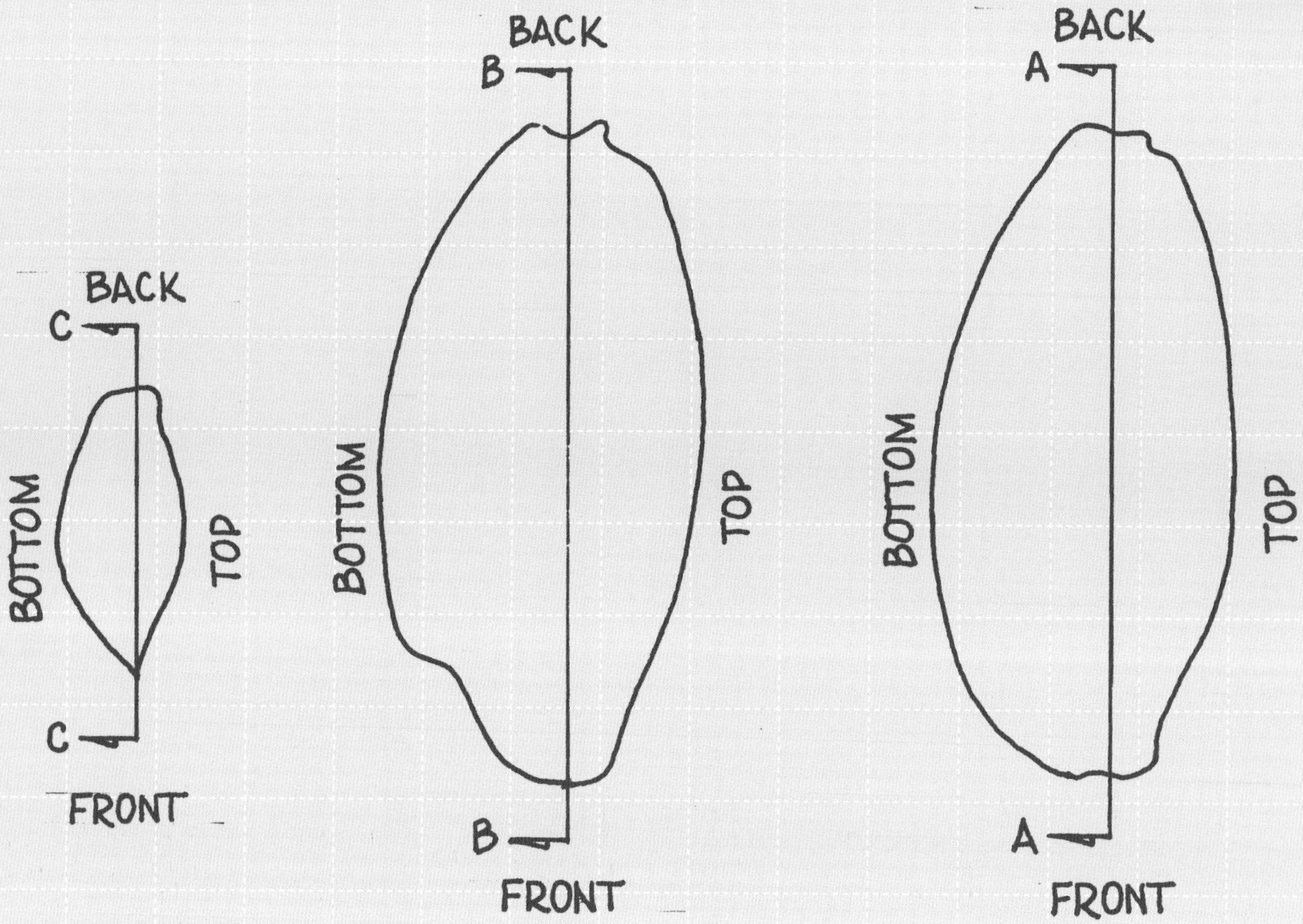

BODY FRONT TO BACK CROSS SECTIONAL TEMPLATES

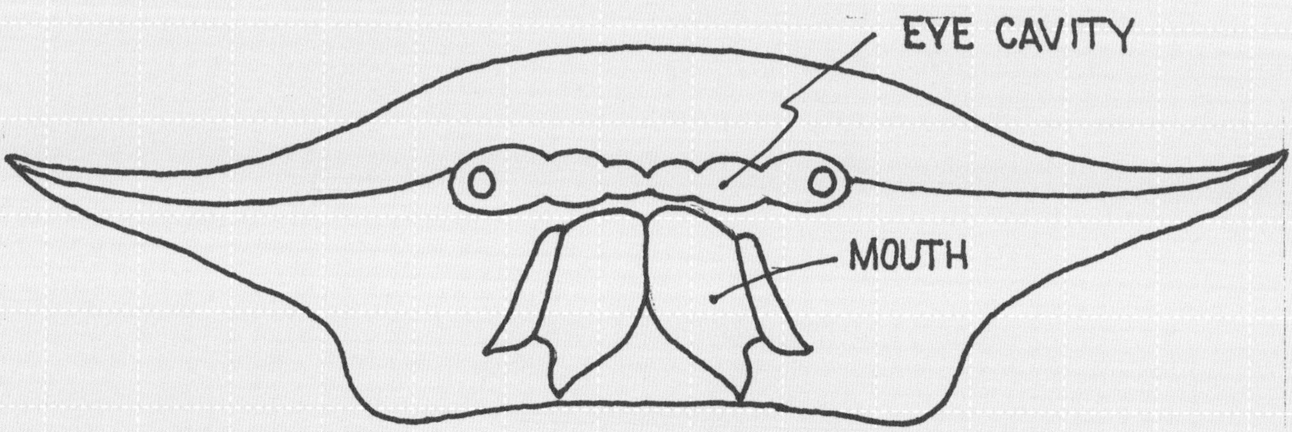

FRONT VIEW

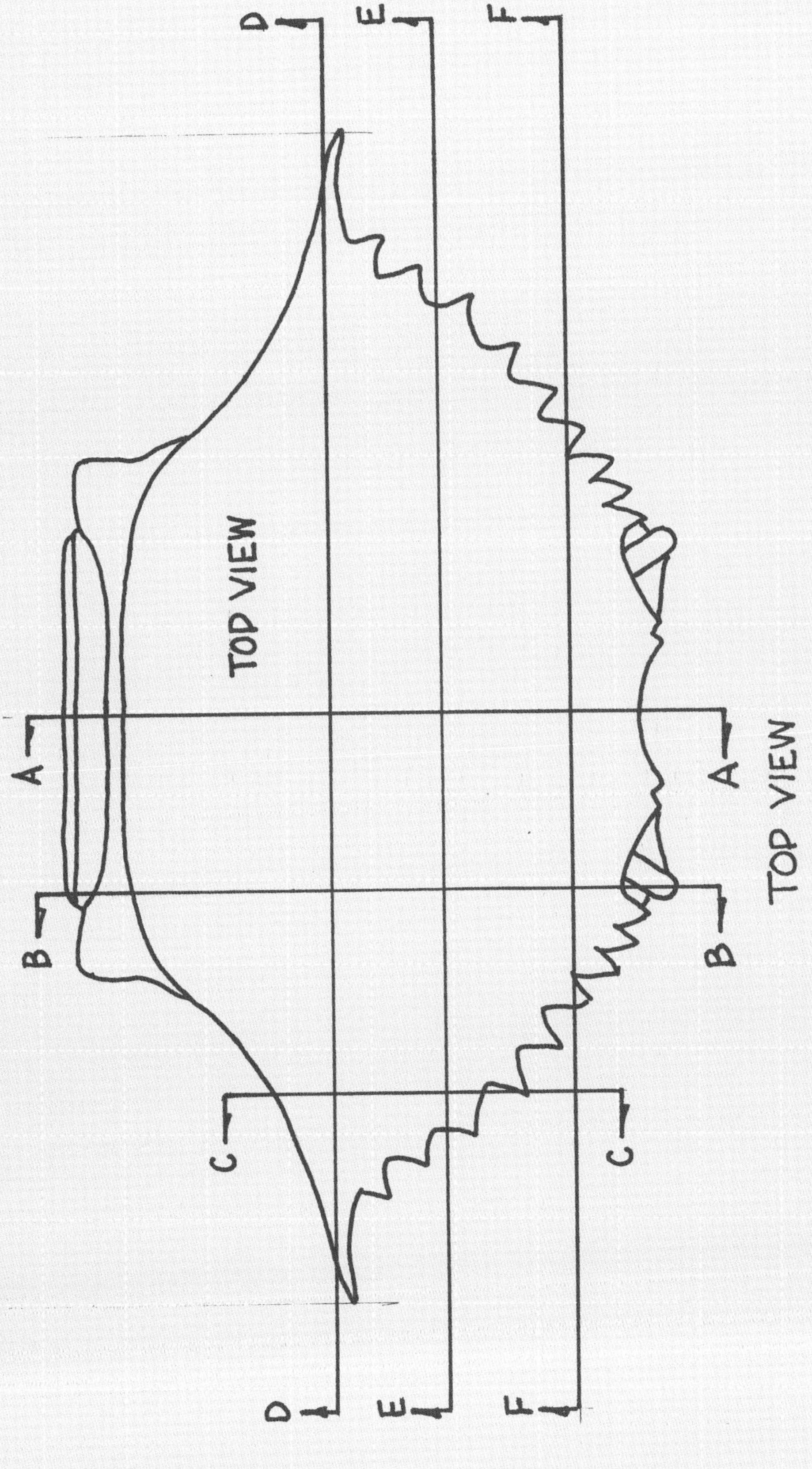
TOP VIEW
TOP VIEW
A
A
B
B
C
C
D
D
E
E
F
F

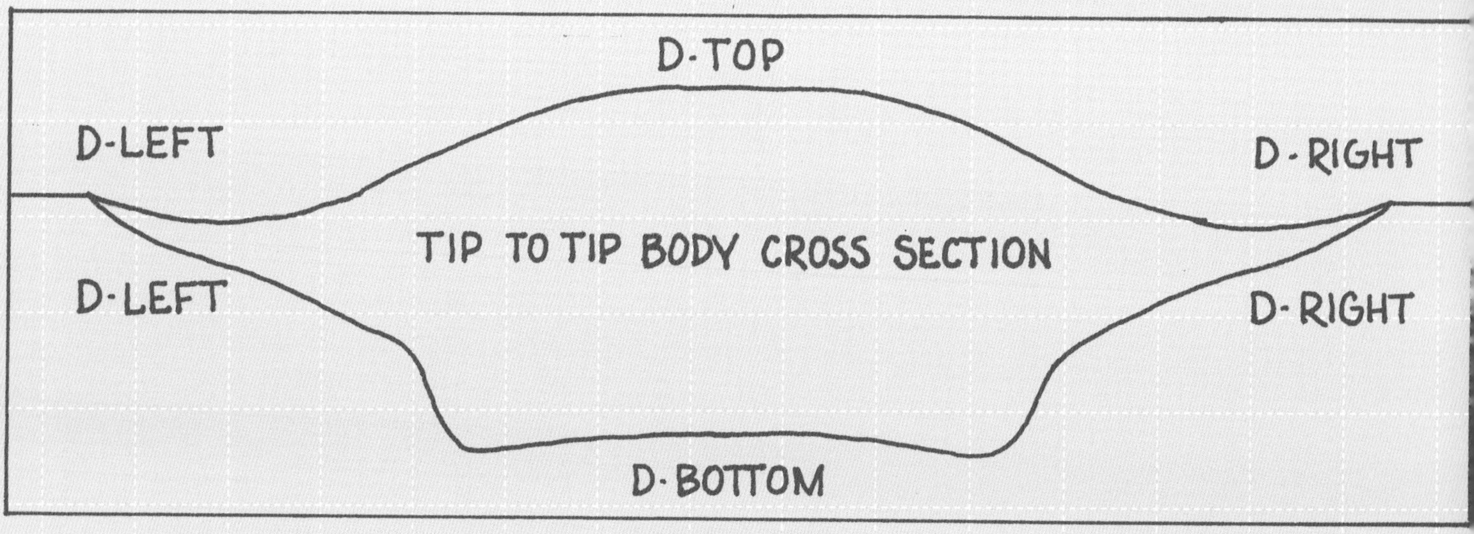
D-TOP
D-LEFT
D-RIGHT
TIP TO TIP BODY CROSS SECTION
D-LEFT
D-RIGHT
D-BOTTOM

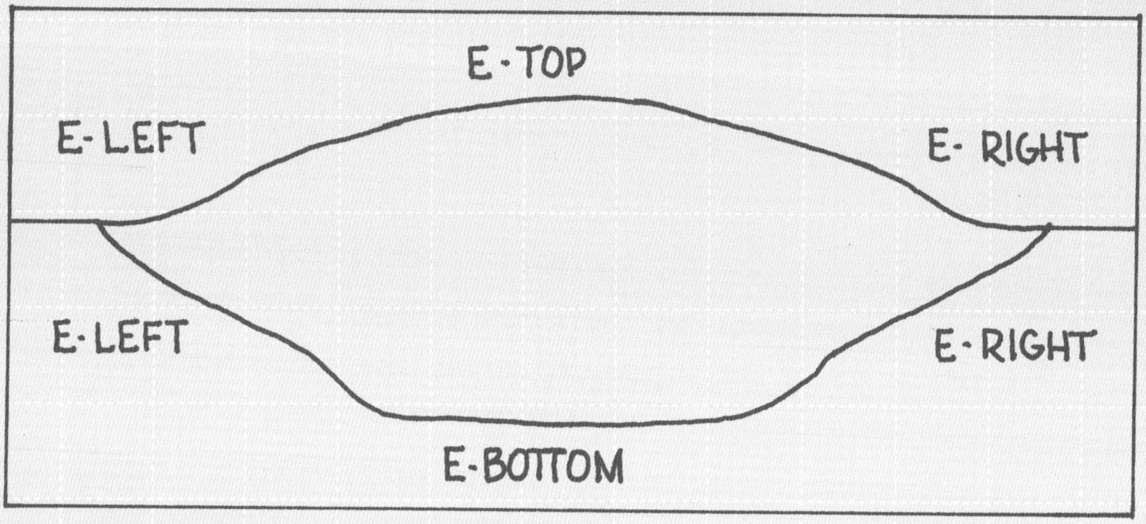
E-TOP
E-LEFT
E-RIGHT
E-LEFT
E-RIGHT
E-BOTTOM

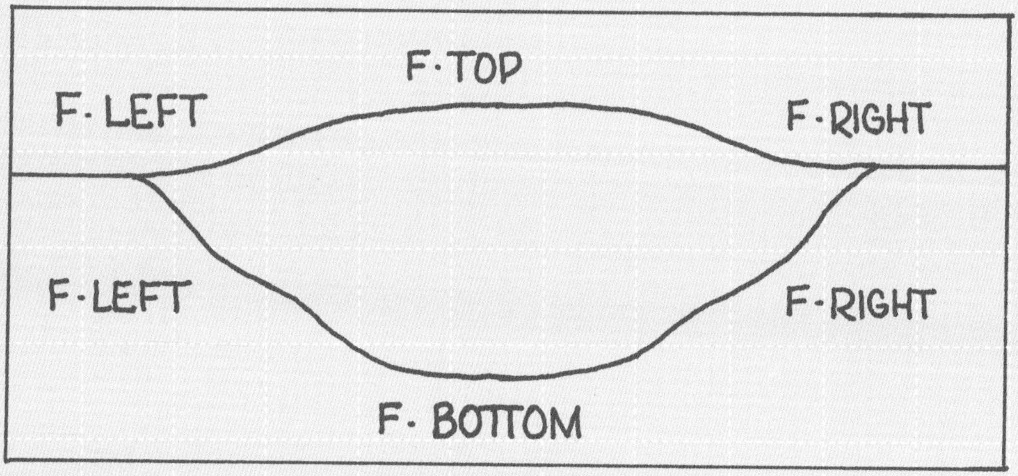
F-TOP
F-LEFT
F-RIGHT
F-LEFT
F-RIGHT
F-BOTTOM

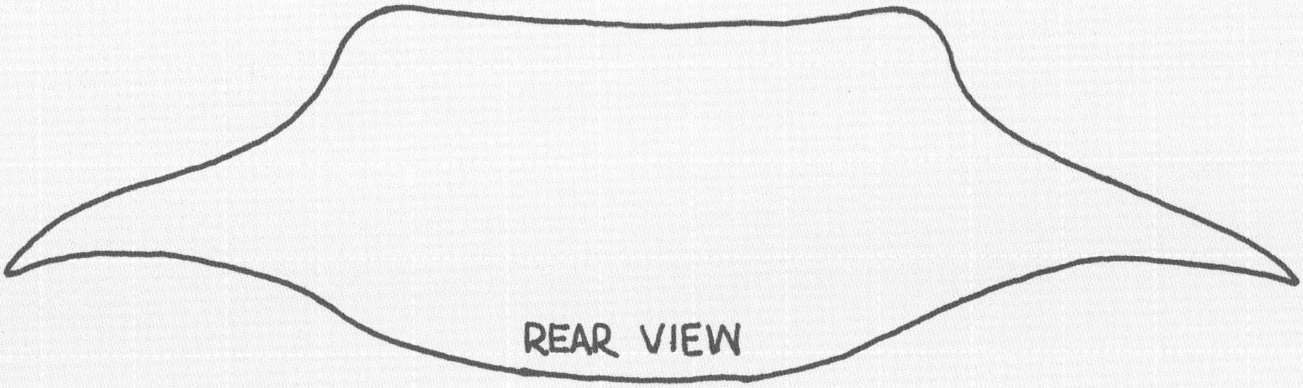

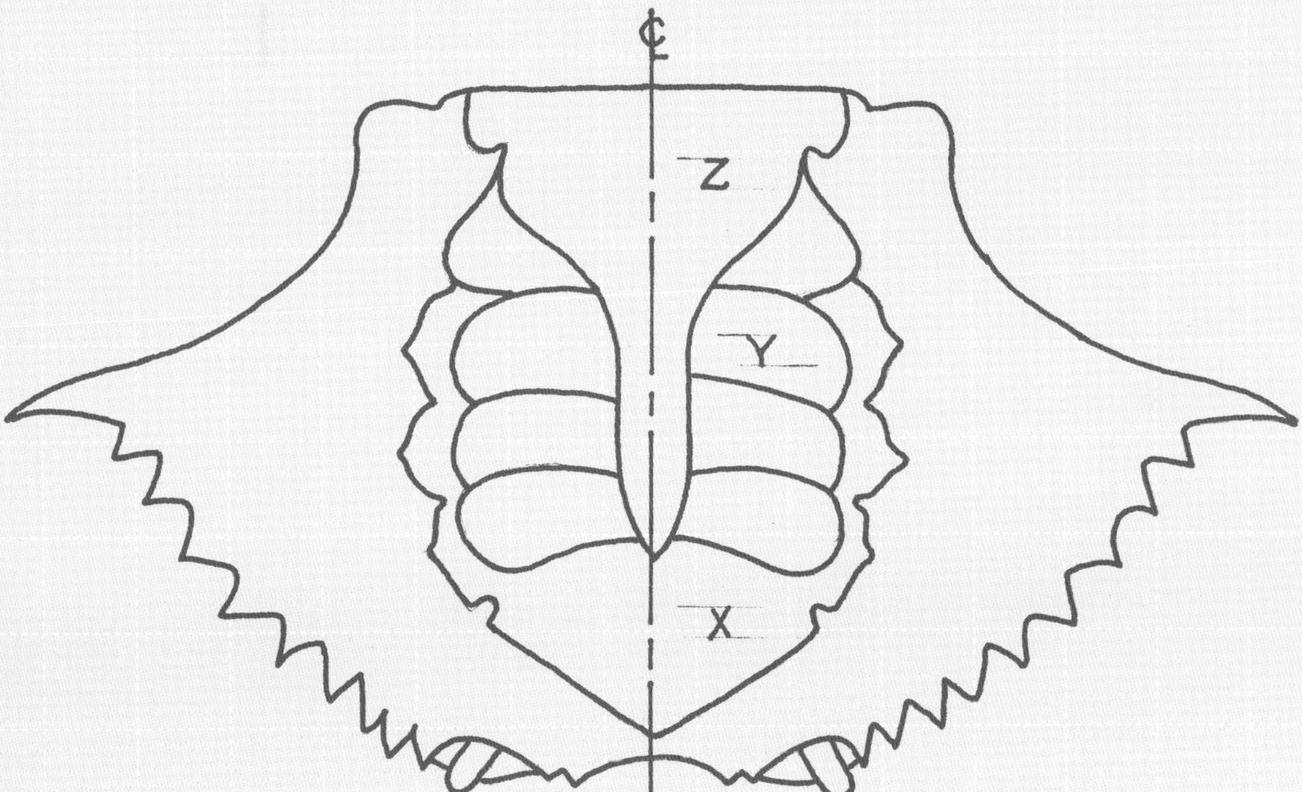

BOTTOM VIEW

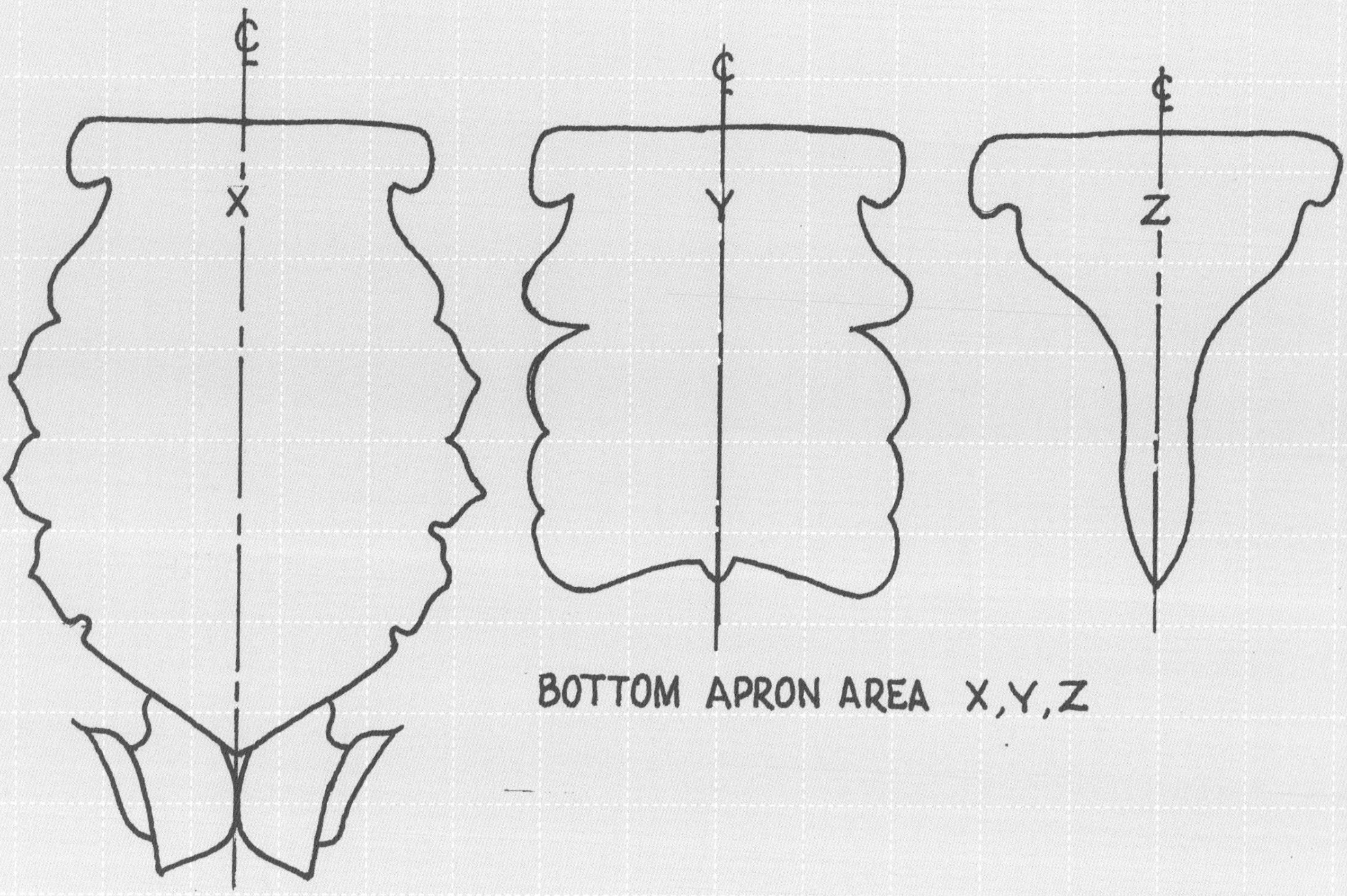

BOTTOM APRON AREA X,Y,Z

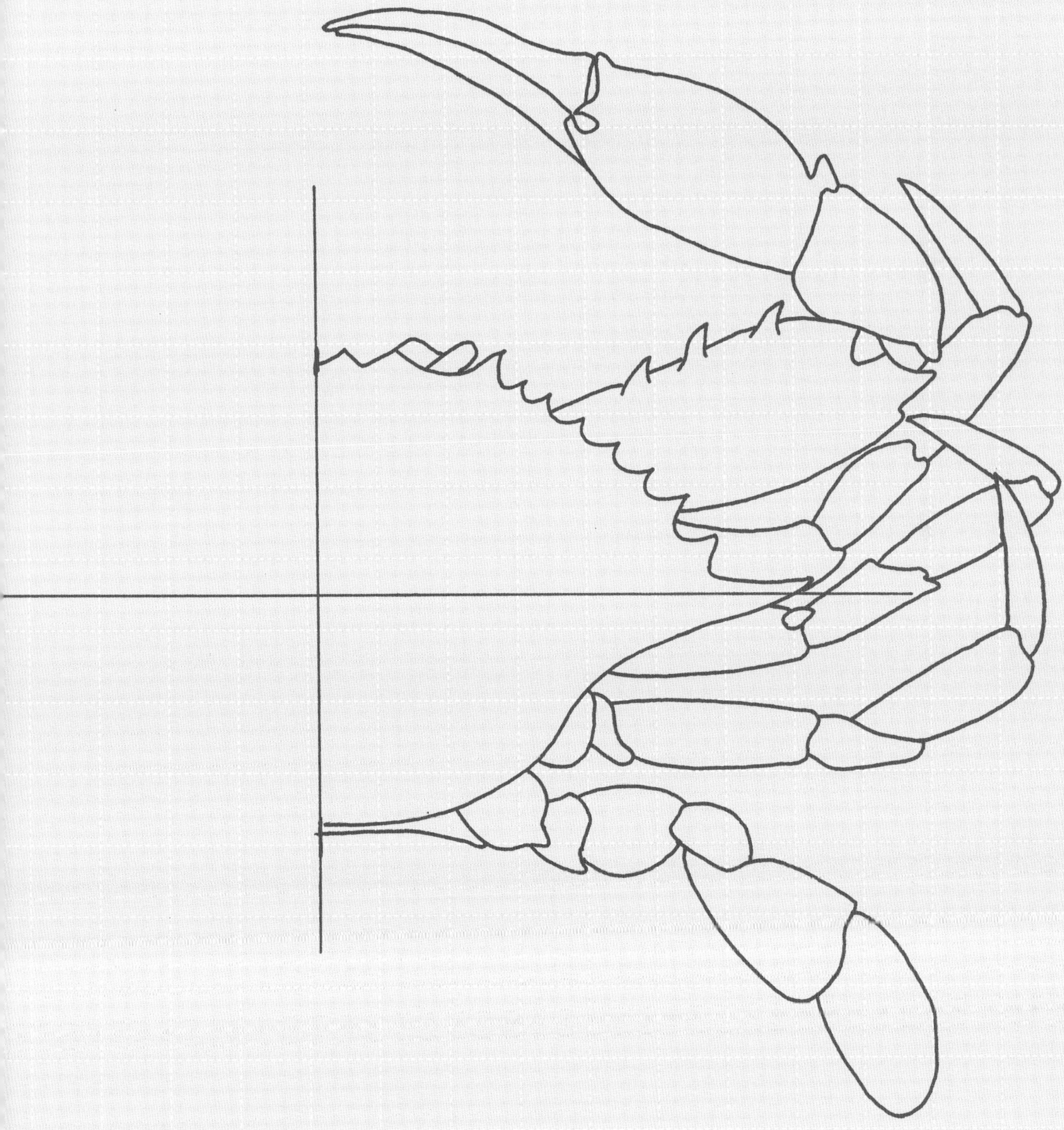

03 | POWER TOOLS vs. HAND TOOLS

I began woodcarving using basic carving tools such as knives, gouges, V-tools, skews, and chisels. All of these tools require hand pressure or use of a mallet to remove wood and carve a project. While hand, non-power tools are still used by the carving purist, many artisans have changed and are now using powered tools as a more comfortable carving technique. Power-carving has opened up the art to more artists who were uncomfortable with the skills necessary in using non-power tools. (Tool hand-sharpening was a unique skill necessary to be successful with hand tools.)

There are pros and cons to both types of carving tools. The advantages I experienced using both methods of carving are:

POWER-CARVING

1. It is more friendly to the arthritic hand and finger joints.
2. It is non-threatening to woodcarvers who struggle with hand-tool sharpening.
3. The wood grain carving direction is of little concern due to the high speed rotation of the bits.
4. Greater detail and depth are achieved through the extensive variety of power bits available.

HAND TOOL CARVING

1. A smoother finished product is possible with little or no sanding when using well-sharpened tools.
2. It is a much less expensive method of carving. A dust collector is definitely necessary and carving bits must be replaced while hand-carving tools will last a life time.
3. Carving tool marks, specifically a gouge, are desired on many finished carvings.
4. Little or no dust and only wood chips are created with hand tools.

Regardless of the tools used, whether they be of power or non-power, there is a place for all woodcarvers in the woodcarving community to express their artistic talents.

Now, to get started with your power-carved Chesapeake Bay Blue Crab you will need the following tools and materials:

POWER TOOLS NEEDED

- **Woodcutting band saw**
- **Floor or bench drill press**
- **WEcheer flexible shaft foot control power-carver**
- **PSI DC 725 three fan dust collector**

MATERIALS NEEDED

- **Tupelo wood**
- **Epoxy carving putty**
- **Epoxy 5-minute adhesive**
- **1/8" dowel rods**
- **A variety of acrylic paints:**

  JoSonja's Gesso
  Deco Art Cinnamon Brown
  Deco Art Deep Red Rouge
  Deco Art Orange
  Deco Art Colonial Blue Light
  Apple Barrel® Apple Antique White

BITS

Carving bits are constructed of various materials such as diamond, carbide, steel, ruby, and ceramic, and come in all kinds of shapes and sizes from coarse to fine. The shapes include Ball, Cone, Cylinder square, Cylinder Radius, Flame, Inverted Cone, Oval, Taper, Tree Point, and Tree Radius. They also come in three shank sizes of 3/16", 1/8", and 1/4".

There are so many types of bits available that it can be difficult to decide which specific bits to purchase. The bits shown here will provide an adequate selection for power-carving the crab and for many of your future carvings as well. Accept the fact that, generally speaking, the more expensive bits will be more effective and last longer, but whatever the bit shape you select, it will sooner or later be the one you need to carve a specific shape.

01

02

03

04

05

06

07

08

09

10

11

12

13

14

01 Marsh sander

02 Ball nose fine blue Typhoon

03 Ball nose course red Typhoon

04 Tapered course Kutzall

05 Inverted cone shape ceramic

06 Tapered carbide cutter

07 Flame carbide cutter

08 Small cylinder carbide cutter

09 Large cylinder carbide cutter

10 Cushioned sanding drum

11 Small ball carbide cutter

12 Small ball Typhoon Burr

13 Pear shape diamond cutter

14 Ball nose fine Kutzall

04 THE CRAB BODY

CUTTING OUT THE BODY

***Author's Note:** To preserve the plans provided in this book it is recommended that you reproduce all drawings to full scale. This can be accomplished by scanning the appropriate drawings on your printer/scanner or getting them reproduced professionally.*

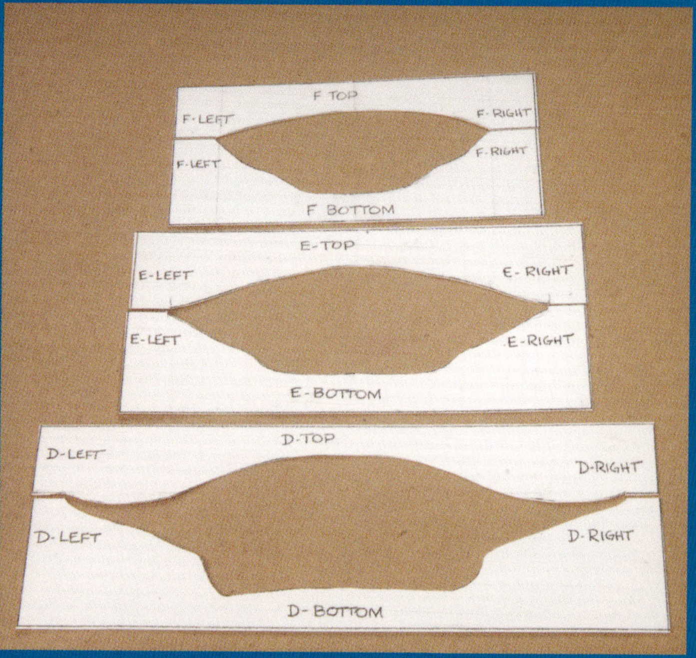

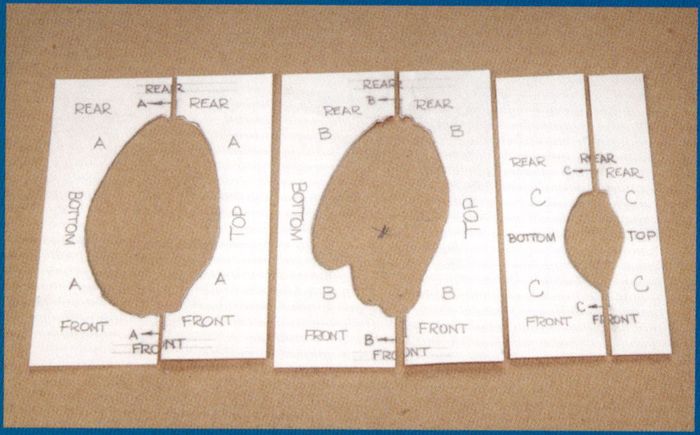

01 To begin the crab body, duplicate the front and top view of the crab body along with the crab body front to back cross-sectionals AA, BB, CC and tip to tip cross-sectionals DD, EE, FF.

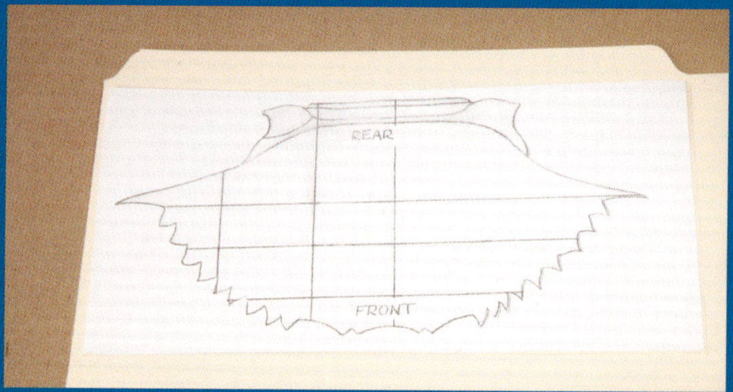

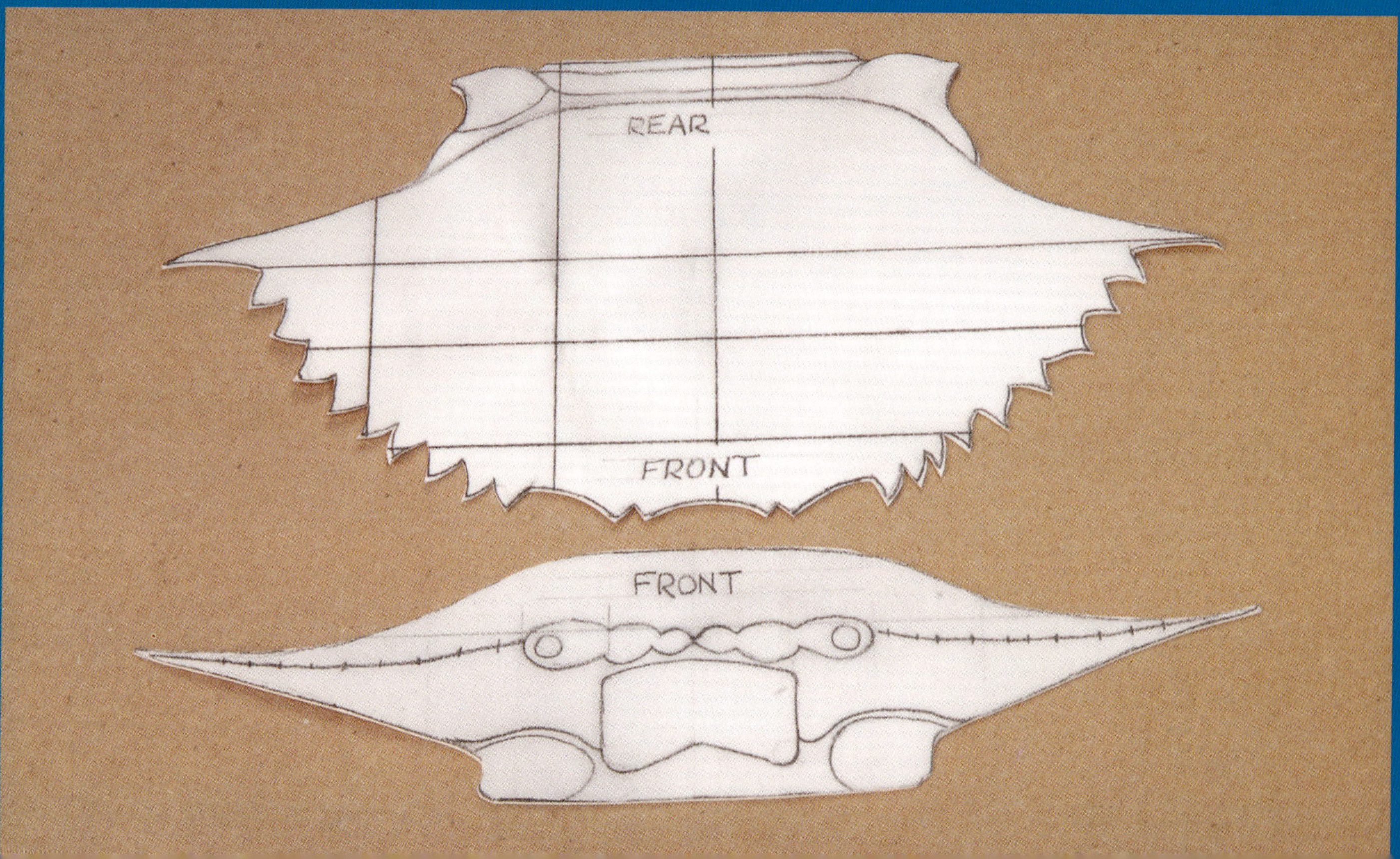

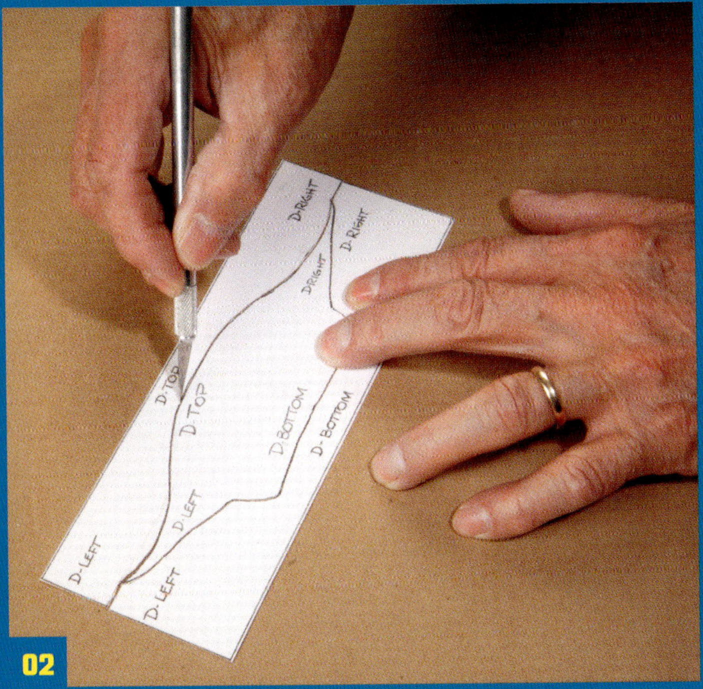

02

Use a sharp box cutter to carefully cut out all the templates.

Carefully and neatly cut out the body parts and cross-sectionals and then label all of the templates to include front, back, left, or right.

03

Using the body top view template and a dark pen or pencil, draw around the template. Make certain there is equal waste on all four edges of the tupelo block.

The block of tupelo carving wood for the body must be a minimum of 2-1/4" thick x 4-1/2" wide x 7-3/4" long. Place the top view of the crab template in the center of the tupelo wood and, with a sharp dark pencil or fine line pen, trace the outline of the crab body. Centering the crab template means that there is waste wood remaining around the entire body to insure safe band saw practices during the cut out.

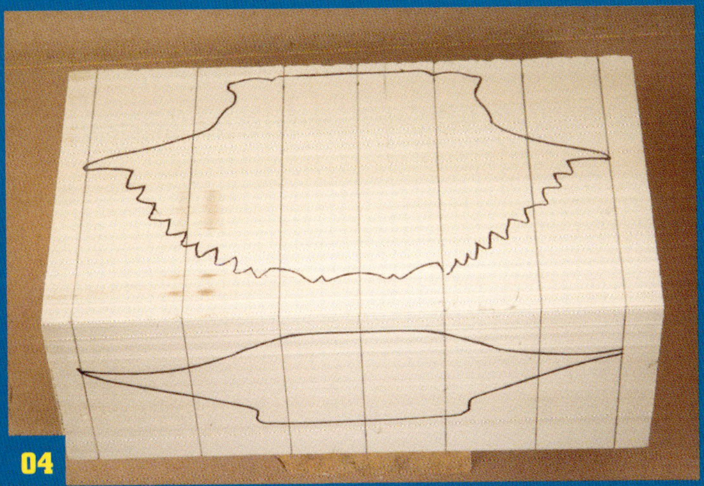

04

Drawing the pencil lines will help insure that both templates are properly located on the tupelo block.

Next, draw a perpendicular line on the wood with a square just touching the crab's right tip (lateral spine). Continue that perpendicular line from the top view to the front view of the block. Transfer the front view of the crab to the tupelo block in a similar manner as was done to the top view, but make certain that the tip of the crab touches the perpendicular line and matches the top view.

05

Cut out the front view first on the band saw, as this is the deepest cut to be made. The band saw cuts are to be made so that the waste material is in one piece and can be taped temporarily for support in cutting out the top view.

The band saw will be equipped with a sharp 1/4" blade. You want to make sure that the blade cutting radius is adequate to rough out the crab body without having to reverse the block material. Cut out the front view of the crab first since the depth of this cut will be the greatest at about 4-1/2" and is the most dangerous. Make certain that the blade guard is set slightly above the height of the wood to insure that your fingers are protected by the guard.

06

Tape the cut out waste piece back together to provide a safe cutting operation.

During cut out, keep the entire waste wood in one piece since this will be taped back together before completing all band saw cutting. When sawing, leave the traced template line on the wood, but do cut very near the line. After cutting out one-half of the crab top view, tape the cut out half back in place before cutting out the other half of the top view to provide a more stable cutting operation. In a similar manner, cut out the second half of the crab top view and again tape both cut waste pieces back in place.

08

The crab body is now completely cut out and removed from the center of the block.

Now cut out the face of the top view, but ignore the eyes (these will be installed separately later). Tape this waste back onto the body and then proceed to cut out the back of the crab's top view. You now have four waste pieces — the crab body blank is ready for power-carving.

Cut out the top view now by lowering the blade guard just slightly higher than the wood and again make the cut so that the waste is in one piece.

07

Cut out the remainder of the top view.

In cutting out the top view, it is necessary to reset the blade guard to slightly higher than the thickness of the tupelo block (about 2-1/2"). Redraw the cut-out lines on the tape if necessary to insure an accurate body blank.

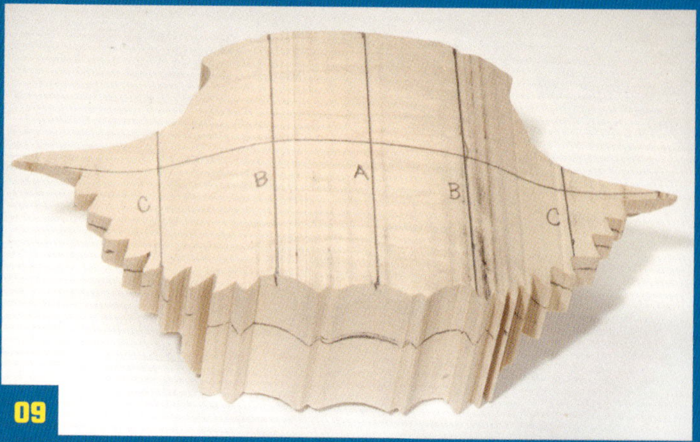

09

Draw all five sectional template lines – C, B, A, B, C – on top of the crab body.

Draw a dark line from tip to tip (lateral spine) completely around the crab body. This line will be used as a reference point for positioning all sectional templates when carving.

POWER-CARVING THE CRAB BODY

The body blank is basically a very square edged object that needs much material removed to round the edges and begin to look somewhat like a crab. For rapid material removal, begin roughing out, using a ball nose coarse Typhoon bit. The body will be shaped using various templates from both front to back and horizontally tip to tip. By carefully carving to match the templates, the crab body will become very realistic, especially when all of the template areas are blended together. Only remove material from the high places when attempting to fit the template.

10

Begin carving station C using a bull nose Typhoon bit. Slowly and carefully remove material.

11

Frequently check the station template to insure a close fit.

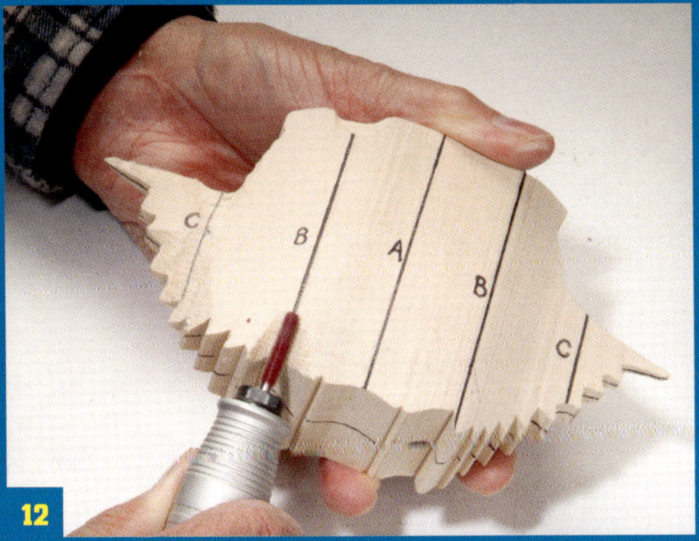

12

After the station C template fits properly, follow the same carving procedure at station B.

13

All five stations are carved to fit the appropriate templates.

14

Carve between each station to blend all five stations together.

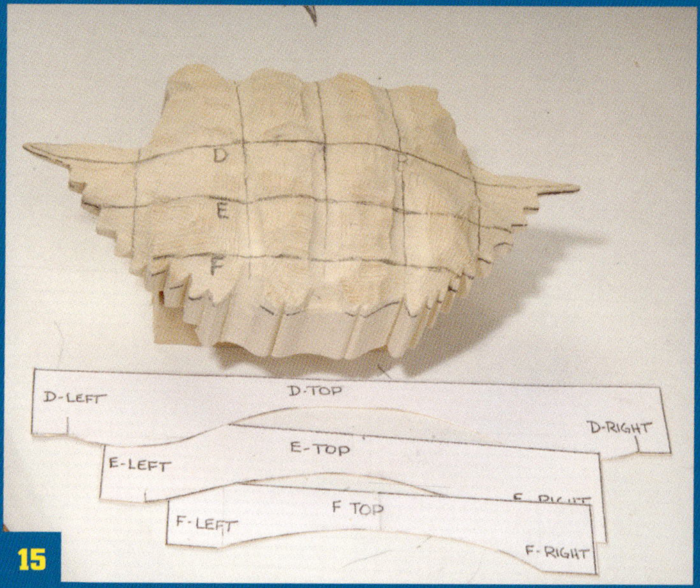

15

Draw horizontal sectional pencil lines D, E, and F on the body and then carve those stations to fit the D, E, and F templates.

16

Blend all stations together using a Kutzall tapered fine bit.

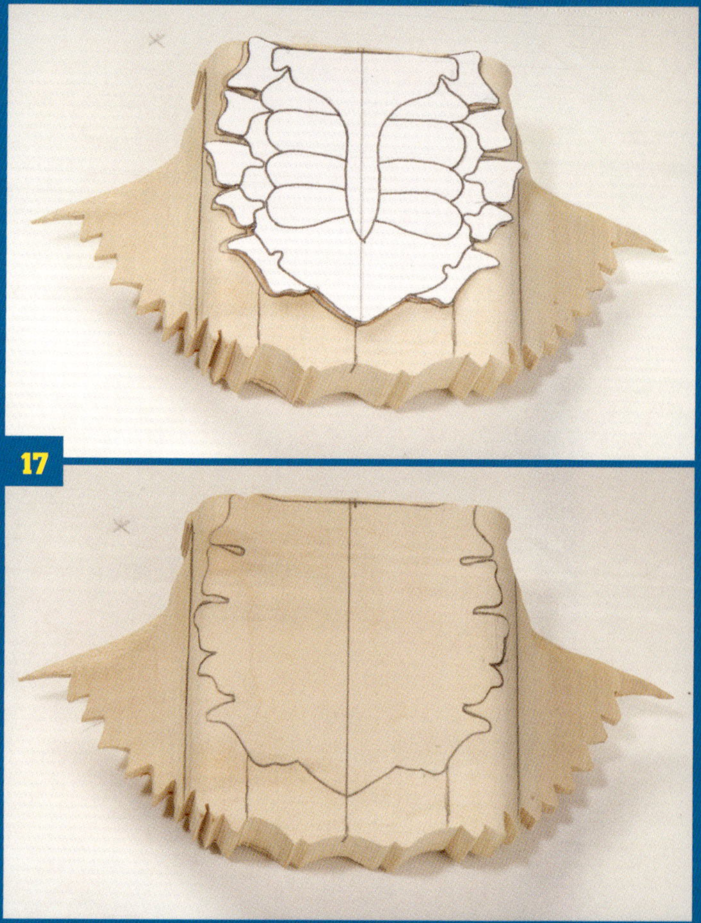

17

Draw the bottom view of the apron on the center line of the crab body.

18

Remove material around the apron area using a cylinder coarse carbide bit and front to back "C" body templates, as was used on the top surface of the crab. Both sides of the crab are carved alike.

19

Smooth the surface area with a Kutzall tapered fine bit.

20

A Kutzall bull nose coarse diamond bit is used to create a slight concave area directly under the shell points (Anterolateral Teeth) on both sides of the body.

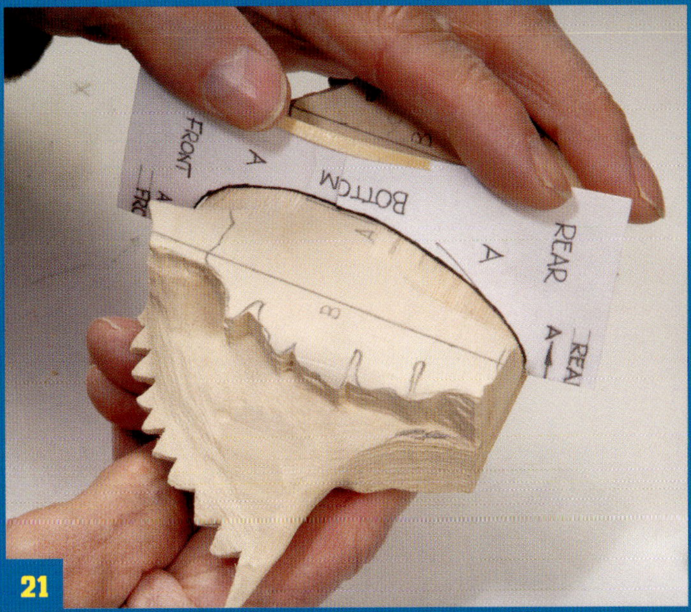

21

Carve stations A and B to fit the bottom body templates of A and B.

22

If too much wood material is inadvertently removed, identify the low area to be built up.

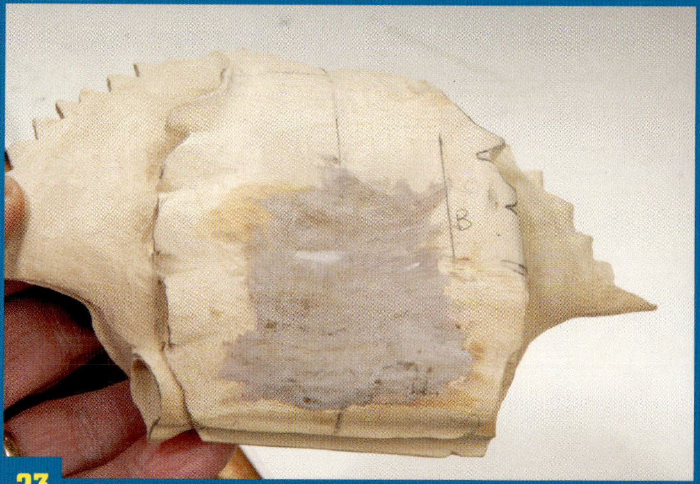

23

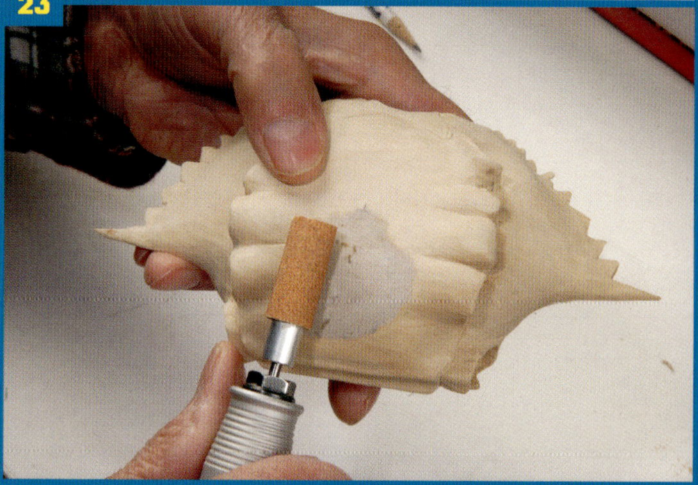

Use an epoxy such as "A plus B Epoxy Putty" to build up the indicated low area and then sand the repaired area to blend in with all of the bottom stations.

24

Carve in the cavities between each leg socket.

25

Sketch the cavity area in all 10 leg sockets and hollow out each socket using a carbide ball bit, leaving a slight edge thickness around the cavity.

26

Using a 150- to 220-grit paper, sand all areas to obtain a smooth surface. This will smooth quickly due to the fact that the tupelo carving wood is very soft.

27

Using the carbide ball bit, hollow out the face area cavities (as shown) on the front view of the plans.

28

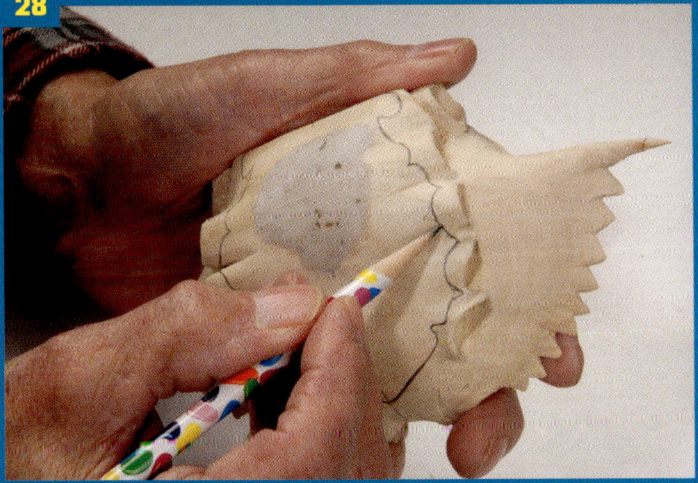

Draw around template X from the plans section. Make certain to line up the center lines.

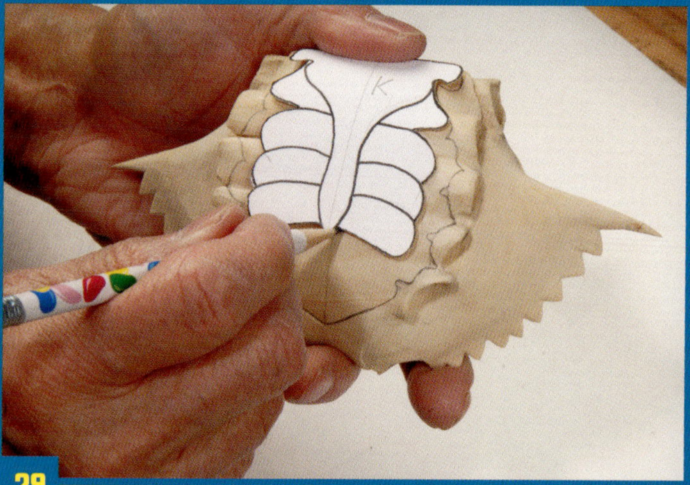

29

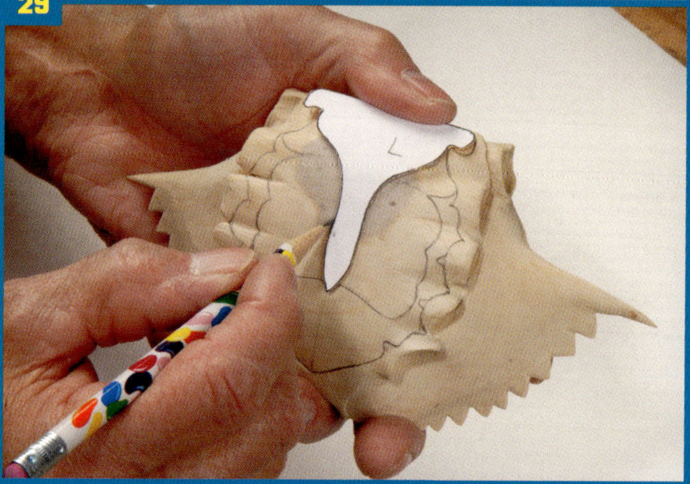

In the same manner, draw around templates Y and Z.

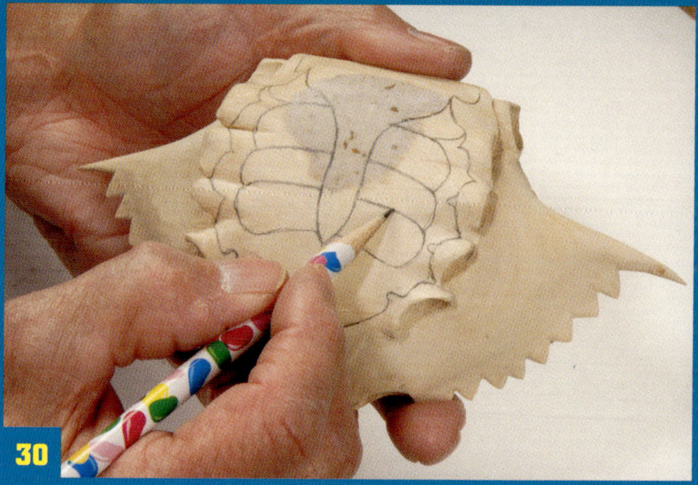

30

All lines are now in place to begin carving the bottom apron area.

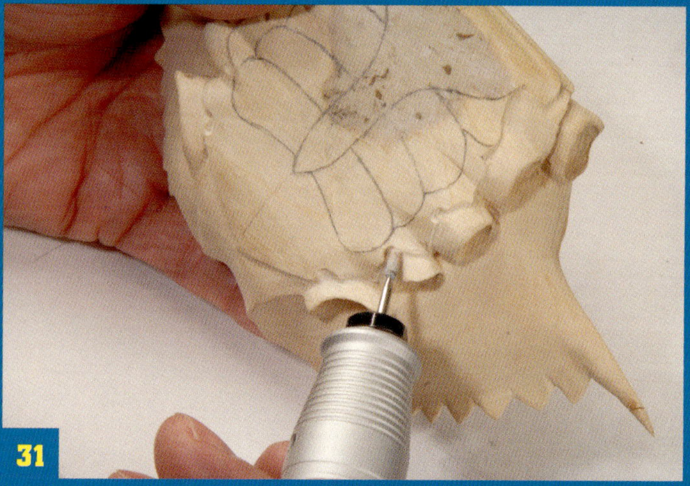

31

Carve a slight depth over top of the leg sockets following the lines of pattern X. The cutter used is a cylinder shaped ceramic bit.

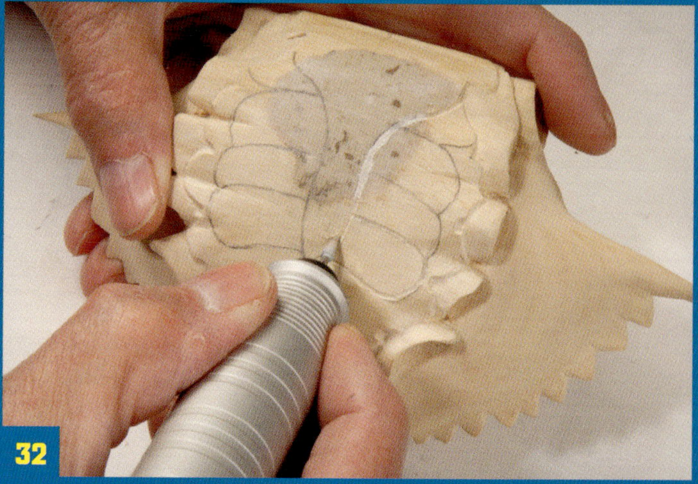

32

Use an inverted cone shaped ceramic bit to carve a "V" indention in both the "Y" and "Z" template drawn areas.

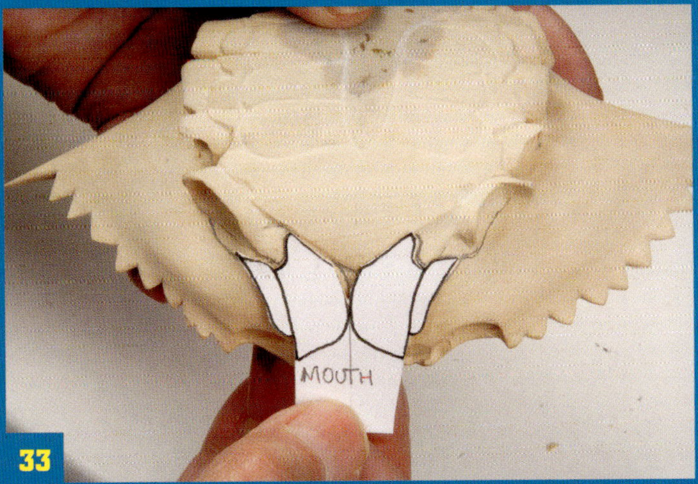

33

Draw the mouth area using the lower part of the "X" template as shown in the bottom apron plan area. The apron and mouth areas can now be carved using an inverted cone ceramic bit to lightly mark the lines previously drawn so that the final appearance is a "V" shaped line.

34

Drill 3/16" holes 1/2" deep in the eye socket area. Angle the drill bit so that it points slightly into the center of the crab body so that the eye when inserted will angle outwardly.

35

Completely round the end of a 3/16" dowel rod with sandpaper and cut the dowel to a length that will allow it to stick out from the eye socket about 1/8".

05 THE MERUS

The crab merus is considered by most eaters of steamed crabs as one of the three most cherished and succulent parts of the crab. The back fin and the propodus part of the claw are equally cherished.

CARVING THE RIGHT MERUS

The right merus is relatively easy to carve and is exactly similar to the left merus. The right merus is identified as the appendage on the right hand side of the crab just as a right arm is identified as an individual's right arm. This identification is carried out throughout this book. Both the right and left drawings are provided for the carver in *Chapter Two*.

01

Cut out the right merus blank using the top and front view drawn on tupelo wood. Draw stations A, B, and C and the top horizontal center line as shown on the plans.

02

Carve the three station areas, checking frequently the template fit and making certain the horizontal center line of the carving matches the center line of the template.

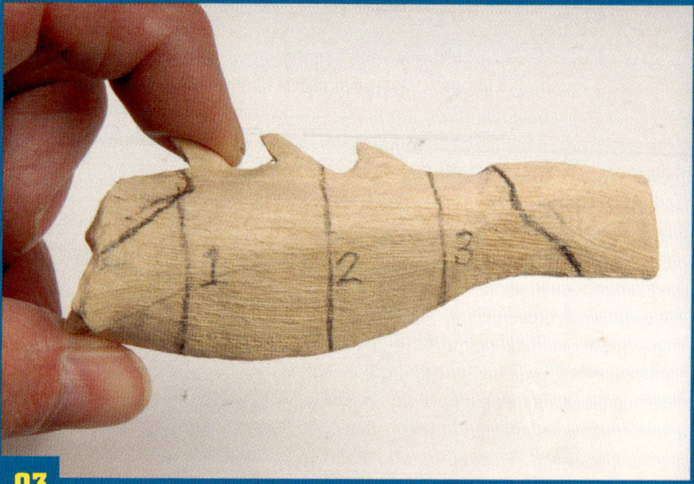

03

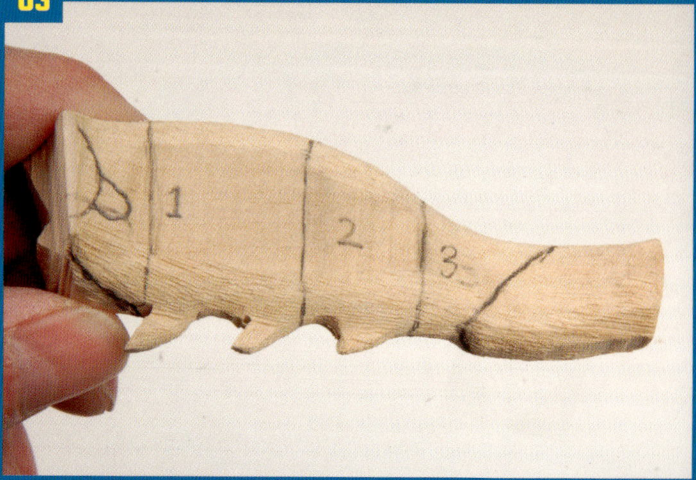

After all the stations are carved and fit the templates, blend all areas between the stations together and redraw the joint lines.

04

Carve in the joint socket areas.

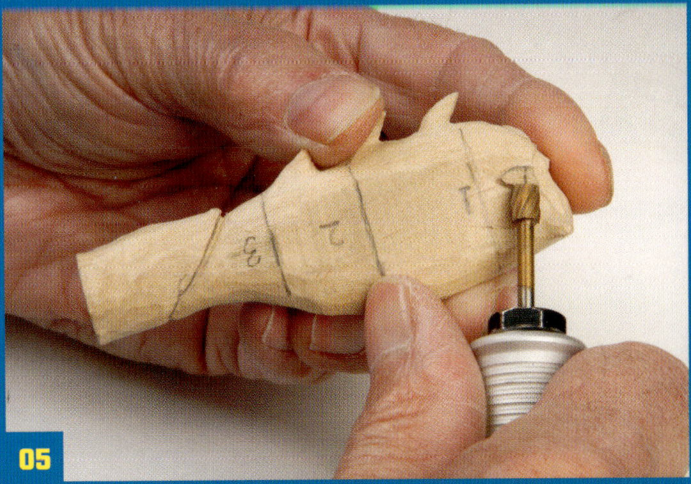

05

Carve in the raised point as shown on the top view.

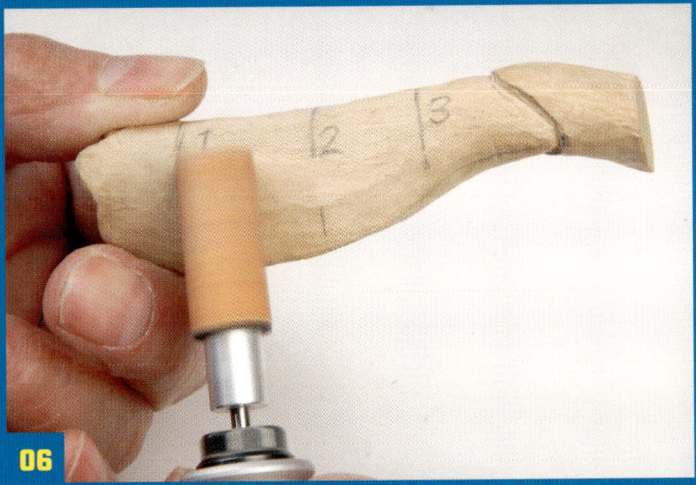

06

Begin sanding using the cushioned sanding drum or sand the merus completely by hand.

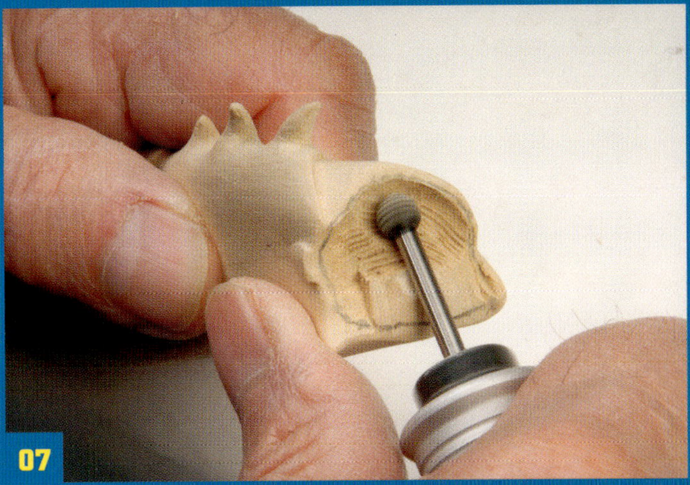

07

Hollow out the end joint using a ball shaped carbide bit.

06

THE CHELA & CARPUS

The Chela and the Carpus are usually considered the claw by most crab eaters. The Chela contains quite a bit of darker crab meat while there is no meat at all in the carpus.

I have kept them together here for ease of carving since the wood grain for the two sections are alike. The same methodology is used to carve the Chela and Carpus as was used in carving the crab body.

CARVING THE LEFT CLAW

Draw both the front and top view on a piece of tupelo wood and cut out both views on the band saw. Reproduce the templates GG, HH, JJ, KK, LL and glue them to a heavier stock of material. Cut out the center section of the template and cut the template in half at the indicated center line. It is important when carving to always hold the template at the appropriate station in a position where the "T" is at the top and "B" is at the bottom of the front view.

Carve each station to fit the template as was done when carving the body of the crab and then blend all stations together. If any of the points were damaged, simply glue another larger point in place of the damaged point and carve it to size and shape. I cut the Dactyl (movable finger) off with a coping saw to make it easier to power carve the teeth and make a concave surface at the base of the teeth. When the carving and sanding are complete, simply dowel and glue the two parts together again.

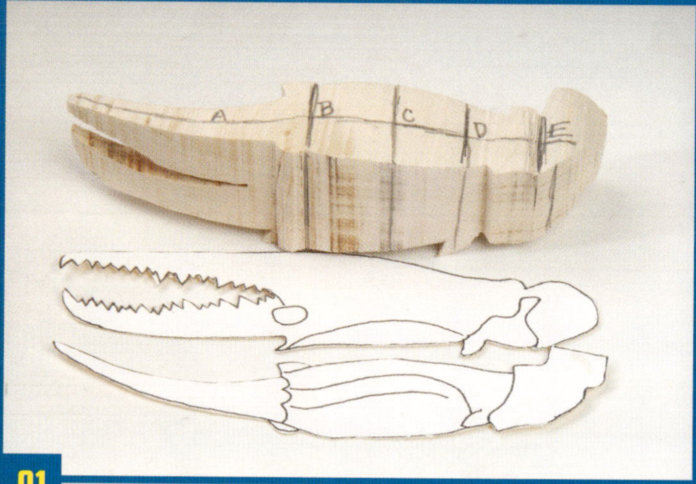

01

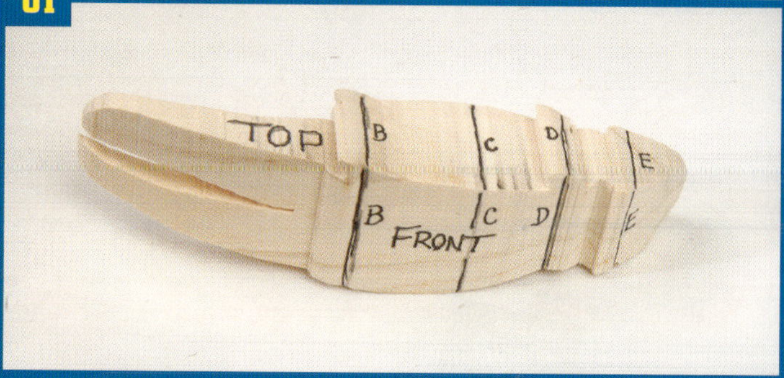

Cut out the left claw on the band saw and sketch stations A, B, C, D, and E and a horizontal center line on the cut out claw.

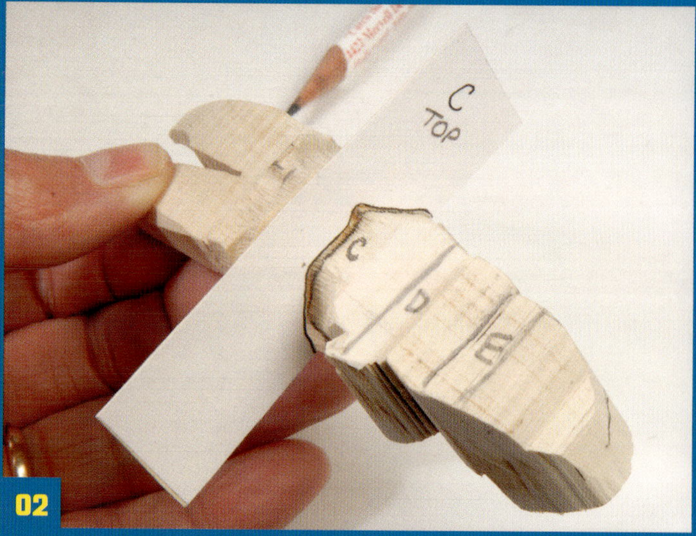

02

Carve the stations slowly. Frequently check the appropriate template to insure a close fit.

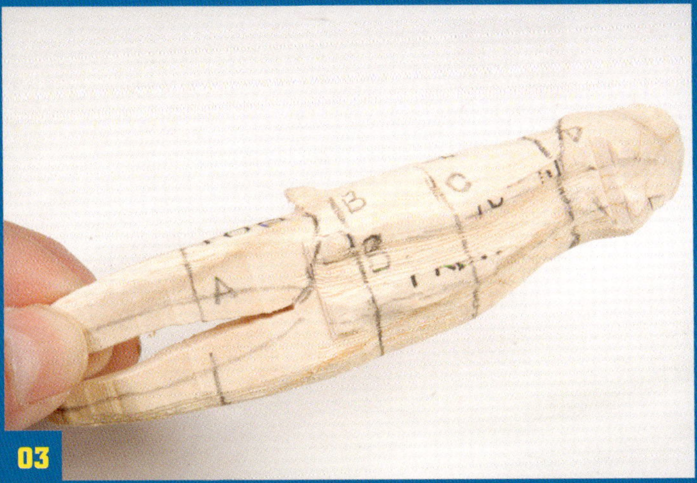

03 After the individual stations are carved, blend in the areas between stations A, B, C, D, and E.

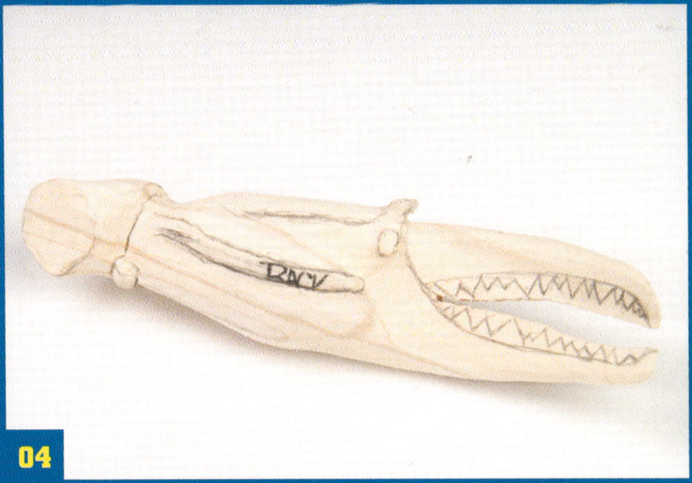

04 Fine carve the joints, points, and both the fixed and movable finger.

05 Cut off the top movable finger with a coping saw to allow space to complete carving both the fixed and movable fingers.

06 Shape the teeth with a cylinder bit and then carve a slight concave area at the base of the teeth using a round carbide or bull nose diamond bit.

CAUTION: Make certain that you use new RIGHT claw drawings and templates when starting to carve the right claw and do not get them mixed up with the previous left claw templates. It will serve you best to put away the previous left claw drawings so that the various templates do not get mixed up.

07 | THE SWIMMING LEGS

The swimming leg of the crab is the paddle, which allows the crab to swim so beautifully sideways. The swimming leg is made up of numerous flexible joints that can move quickly in all directions thereby allowing the crab to be very fast and illusive. The plans for the swimming legs are drawn showing the legs in a very normal position.

CARVING A SWIMMING LEG

01

Transfer the right swimming leg drawing onto a 3/8" thick tupelo and the end leg paddle to 1/8" thickness wood. Cut out the two pieces on the band saw.

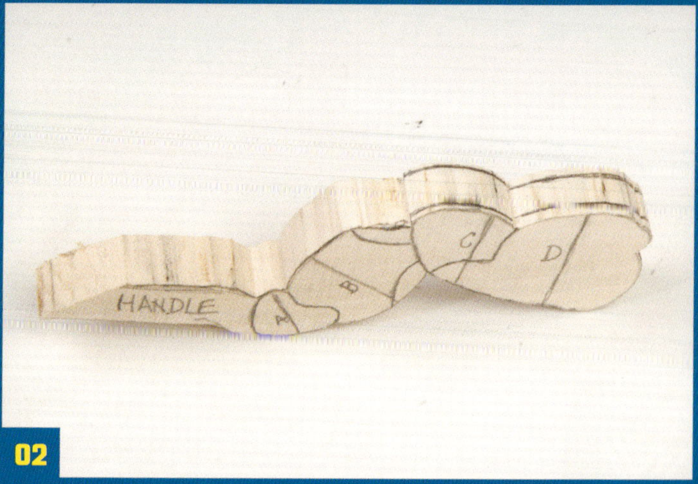

02

Draw in all joint lines and the template stations A, B, C, and D on the 3/8" thick leg.

03

Reduce the thickness between the joints using the sectional templates AA, BB, and CC.

04

Round all edges using the sectional templates AA, BB, and CC as a guide and redraw all joint markings.

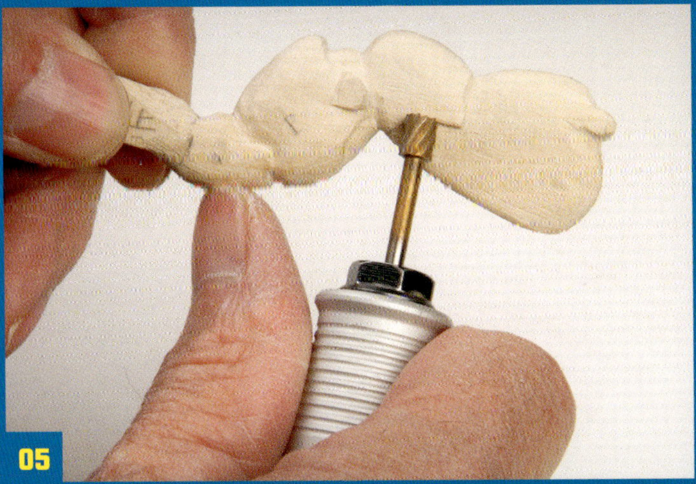

05

Using a cylinder carbide bit, carve in all joints and raised points.

06

Sand thoroughly the entire swimming leg with 150-grit sandpaper. Keep the joint edges sharp.

07

The 1/8" thick end leg paddle can be tapered at the edges using template AA as a thickness guide.

08

Carve out the area on the paddle about 1/16" deep. The same carving procedure will be done on the swimming leg where the two pieces fit together creating a half joint.

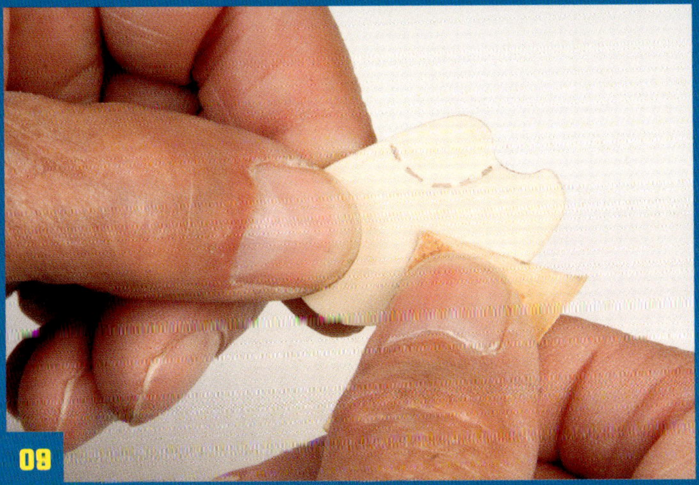

09

Sand the paddle completely.

10

The tip AA will fit under the leg BB, making a half joint. Glue together at that joint.

08 THE WALKING LEGS

All six walking legs (3 left and 3 right) are very similar to one another in shape and only differ in size. Most of the differences that you see are the positions that the crab moves them. Each joint is very flexible and mobile, which allows the crab the ability to grasp or hold onto most any irregular shape. These flexible legs are vital to the crab when walking, holding food, or carrying a female crab during the long mating process.

The legs shown in the plans are drawn as they are generally seen on crabs. However, feel free to change any one of the leg joints to obtain the artistic effect you want to achieve. The end tip joint is extremely flexible with at least a 90-degree movement. Even the joint where the leg attaches to the body has great movement.

When carving the legs and planning how the crab will be finally mounted, take the liberty to design the legs to help you create a unique final mounting. The plans show a number 1, 2, and 3 right walking legs with the leg closest to the claw #3 Left and #6 Right being slightly larger than the other walking legs.

CARVING THE WALKING LEG

Using the band saw and scrap tupelo, rip a 1/8" and 3/8" thick pieces of wood for carving all six walking legs.

01

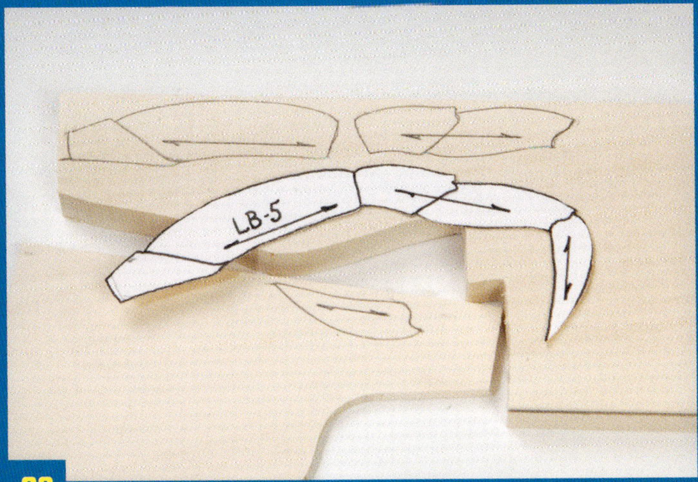

02

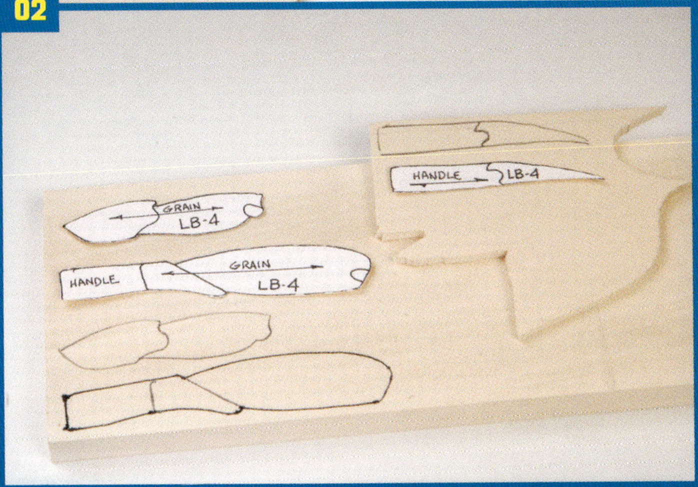

Draw template LB-5 onto the 3/8" and 1/8" wood pieces, making certain that the arrow on the template matches the grain of the wood. The two larger pieces are 3/8" thick and the small tip is to be cut from 1/8" stock.

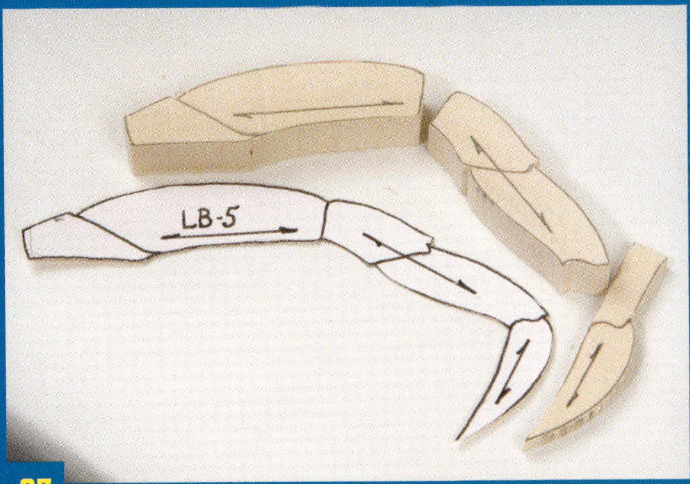

03

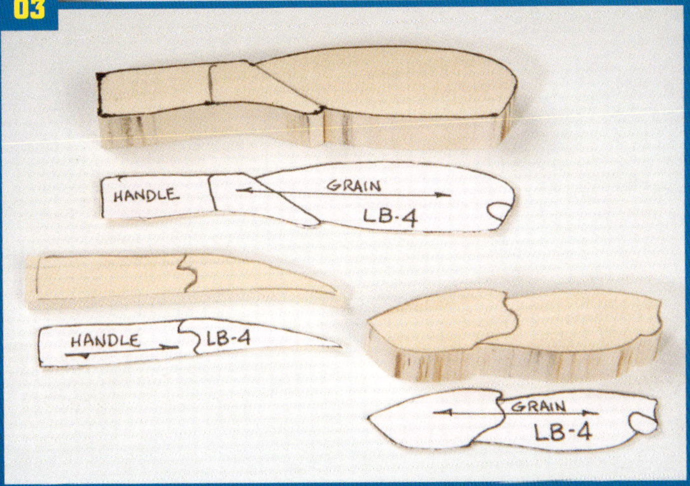

Cut out the three parts of LB-5 and LB-4 on the band saw. An extension is included on the tip to serve as a handle for this small piece.

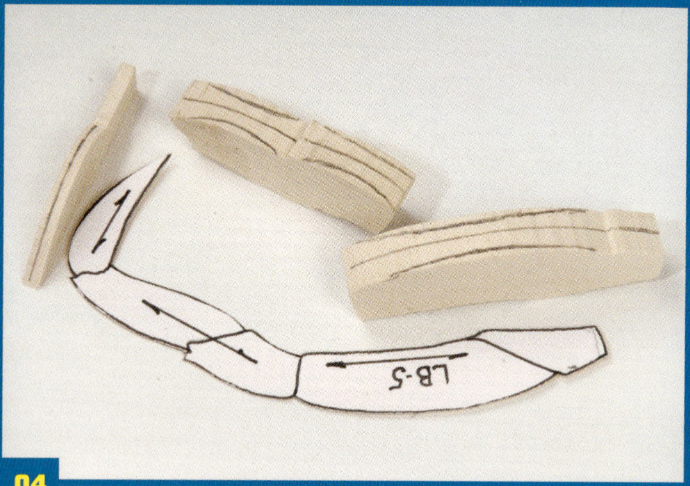

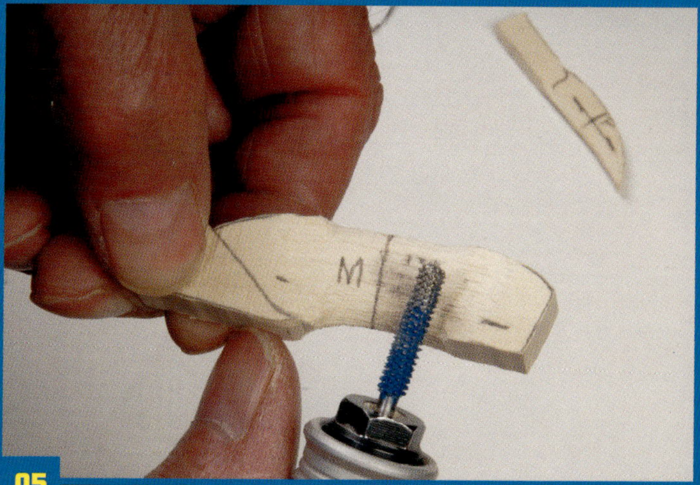

04

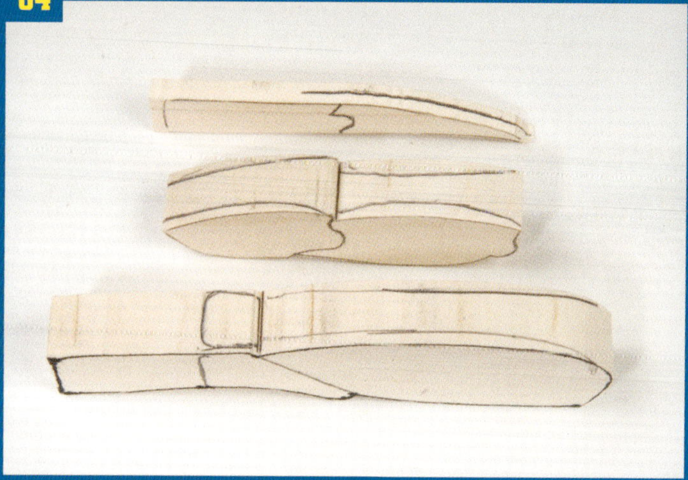

Sketch the leg top view thickness lines.

05

Using a ball nose fine Typhoon bit, carve the leg thickness and begin rounding all edges to fit the sectional templates.

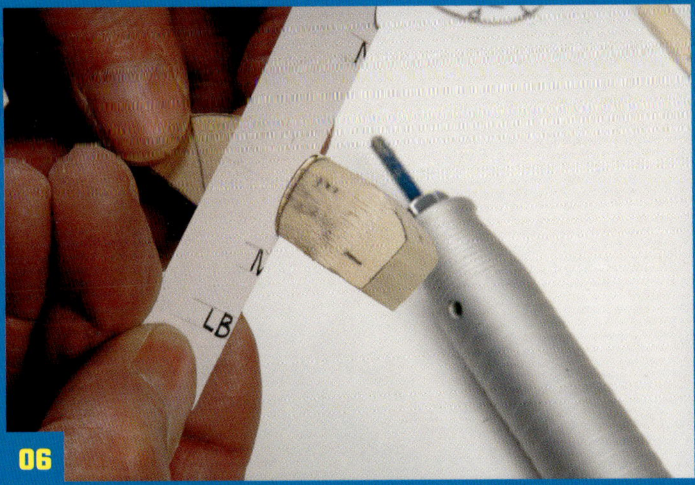

06

After rounding the edges, fine tune the carving by frequently checking the sectional template fit at station M.

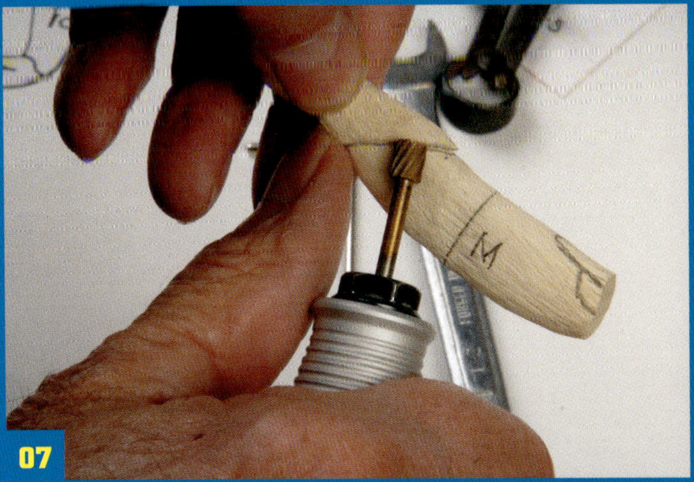

07

Using a coarse carbide cylinder cutting bit, carve the four joint lines that identify each leg joint.

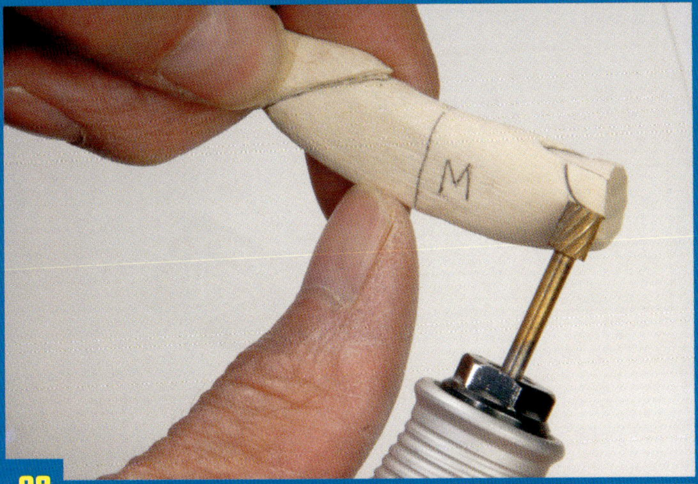

08

09

A "V" shaped joint cavity located between joints M and N is carved about 1/16" deep, which allows for a very flexible joint movement on the live crab.

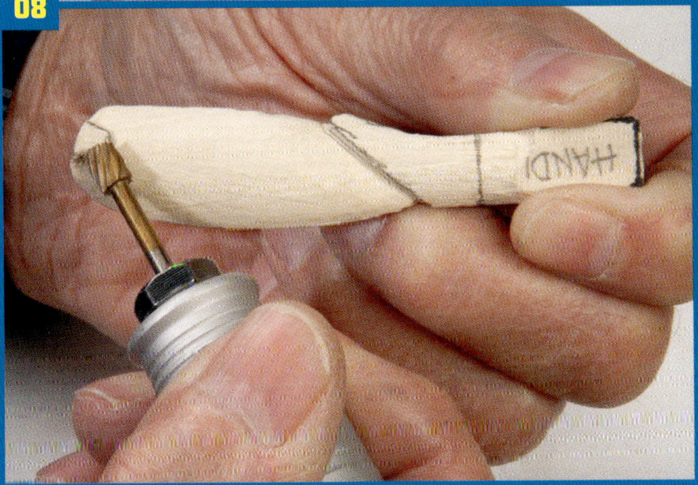

The "V" shaped points are also edged with the cylinder cutting bit to lower the area around the "V" point and make the point slightly raised.

10

Sand all areas of the carved leg with 150-grit sandpaper, but make certain that the edges are not rounded.

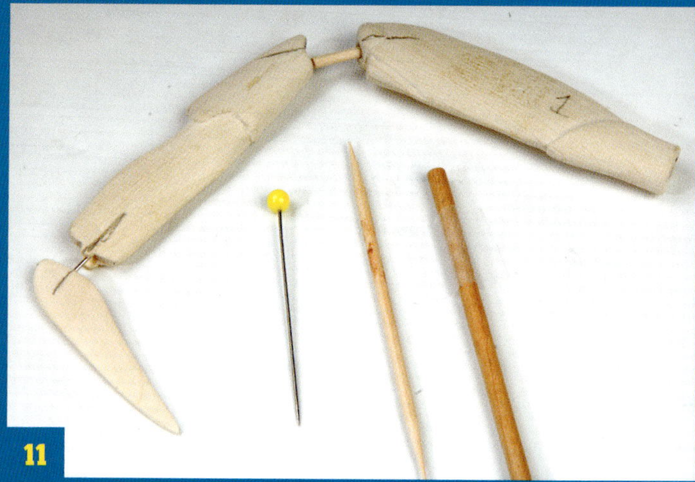

11

Pin parts together in the desired location with a pin, round toothpick, or a 1/8" dowel rod.

12

Glue the dowel joints together with a 5-minute epoxy. Hold the glue joints in the desired position until the epoxy hardens. A pencil-drawn marking on both pieces to be attached will help with the correct drilling angle.

The completed leg LB-4.

13

PAINTING YOUR CARVING

09

Observe the photographs of the live crab body to assist you in not only your color selection, but also the proper location of those colors. The selected colors in this book were thinned and blended with other colors to realistically match the real crab.

THE CRAB BODY

Underside view of a male crab with all pereopods shown.

Top view of a male crab with all pereopods shown.

Rear view of the crab body.

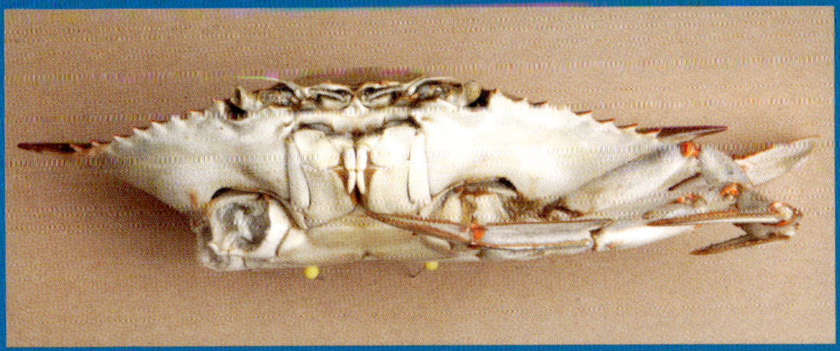

Front view of the crab body.

01

The crab body is painted Antique White after first painting a primer coat of Jo Sonja's Gesso acrylic paint.

02

Paint the top of the crab body with a blend of Cinnamon Brown and Bright Yellow acrylic paint. Paint the crab body points a Deep Red Rouge.

03

Using a sharp pointed toothpick and Off-White paint, place numerous dots over the lighter front surface of the crab body.

04

Once painting is complete of all the crab parts, mount each part on a scrap piece of wood so that they can be sprayed in all directions. The live crab has a slight sheen and should be lightly sprayed with at least three coats of Minwax® clear semi gloss or satin polyurethane spray finish.

THE CLAW

Bottom view of the left cheliped.

Top view of the left cheliped.

Outside view of the left cheliped.

Inside view of the left cheliped.

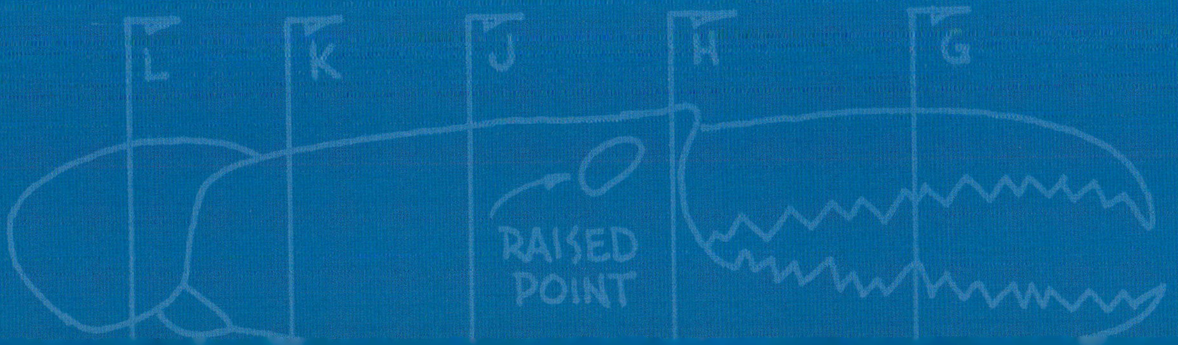

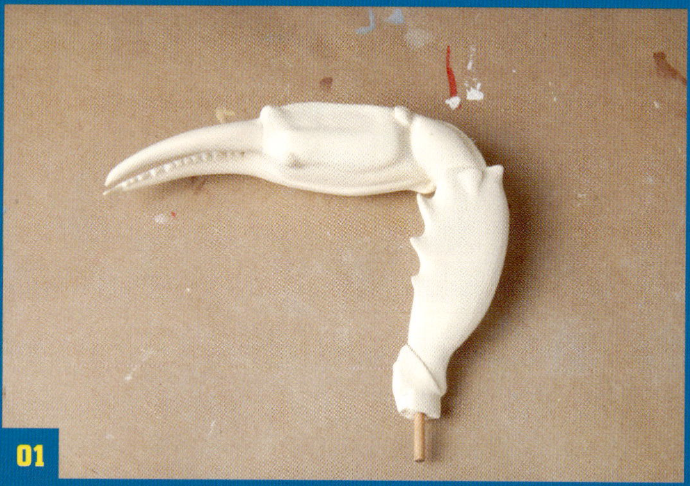

01

The cheliped is painted an Antique White after first painting a primer coat of Jo Sonja's Gesso acrylic polymer.

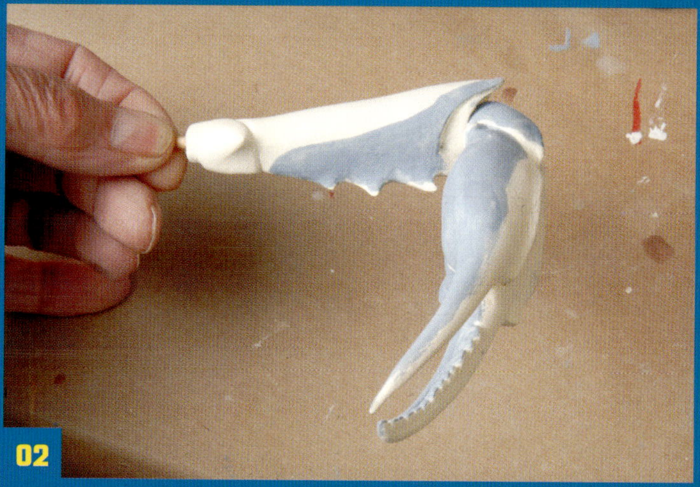

02

Paint a very light, thin coat of Colonial Light Blue on all blue areas.

03

Paint a very light, thin coat of Cinnamon Brown with a touch of Yellow to blend the brown to an olive drab color.

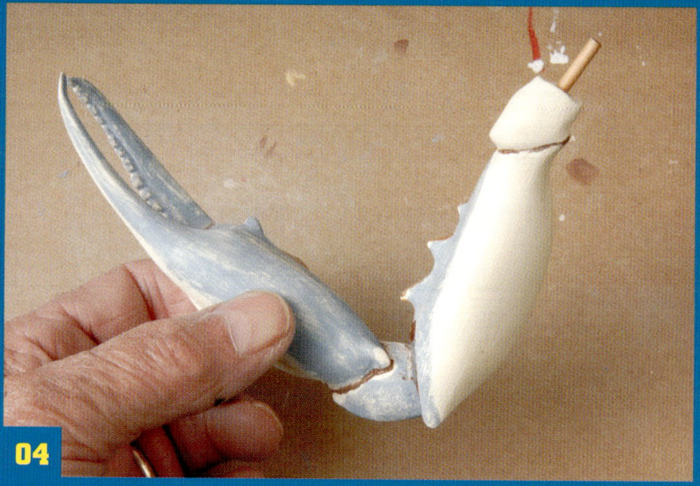

04

Paint Cinnamon Brown in each joint to outline and identify each moving joint.

05

A Deep Red Rouge is used to paint all raised points and pincher teeth. Use a pointed toothpick to add varying spotted points of off-white paint all over the pincher.

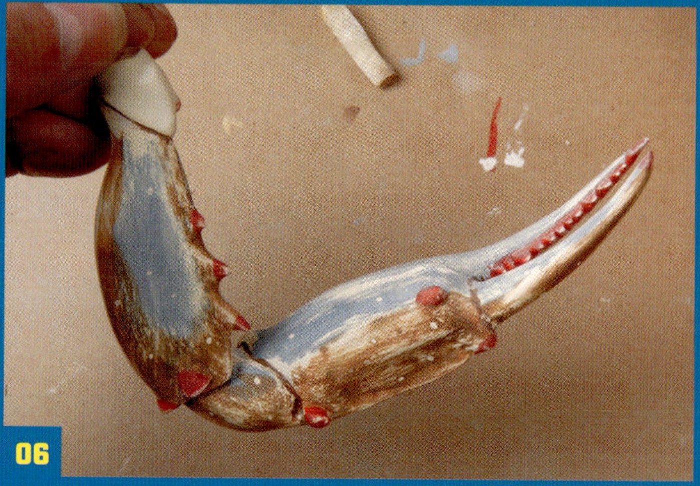

06

Lightly sand and blend all colors using a fine 3M pad or 400-grit sandpaper.

A SWIMMING LEG

Underside view of the swimming leg.

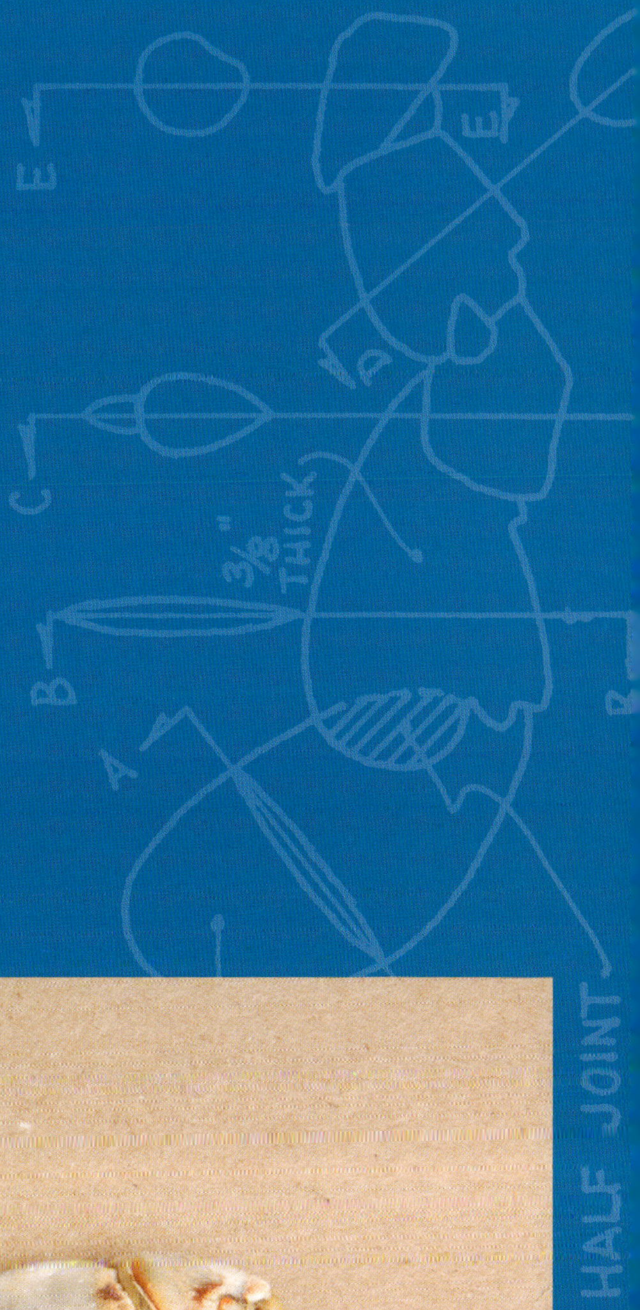

Top view of the swimming leg.

01

Thoroughly sand the swimming leg with a fine grit (220) sandpaper and insert a dowel at least 2" long into the end of the leg to act as a handle for the entire painting process. Paint the entire leg with a base coat of Jo Sonja's Gesso acrylic paint as a primer to produce a smooth, matte white surface for additional acrylic colors.

02

Sand the Gesso primer lightly again and then paint the entire surface with an antique white acrylic paint.

03

The raised heart-shaped areas at the various joints are to be painted an Orange/Red color. I have mixed a small amount of Orange with a larger amount of Deep Red Rouge to duplicate this color. Any additional paint to be removed can be done with light sanding.

04

Paint a fine line (Cinnamon Brown) in all four joints and immediately remove all paint excess with a piece of damp cloth or wet Q-tip®. Dry acrylic paint is removed with light sanding so that only a thin line between the joints remain.

05

Paint a lightly thinned coat of Colonial Blue over the upper half of the swimming leg, feathering it out into the lower half of the Antique White with a damp cloth or Q-tip®. After drying, a light sanding with 220 or finer grit paper will additionally feather and blend in the Colonial Blue with the Antique White.

06

In a similar manner, paint a very thin coat of Cinnamon Brown on the top edges of the swimming leg and feather the brown paint into the Colonial Blue again with a damp Q-tip® or light sanding. Adding very thin color coats and sanding can be applied many times to get the desired results.

The final painted swimming leg.

THE WALKING LEGS

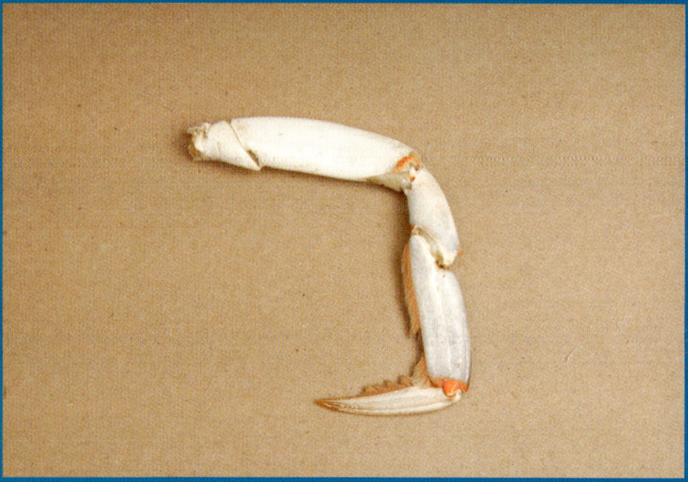

Bottom view of the right walking leg.

Top view of the right walking leg.

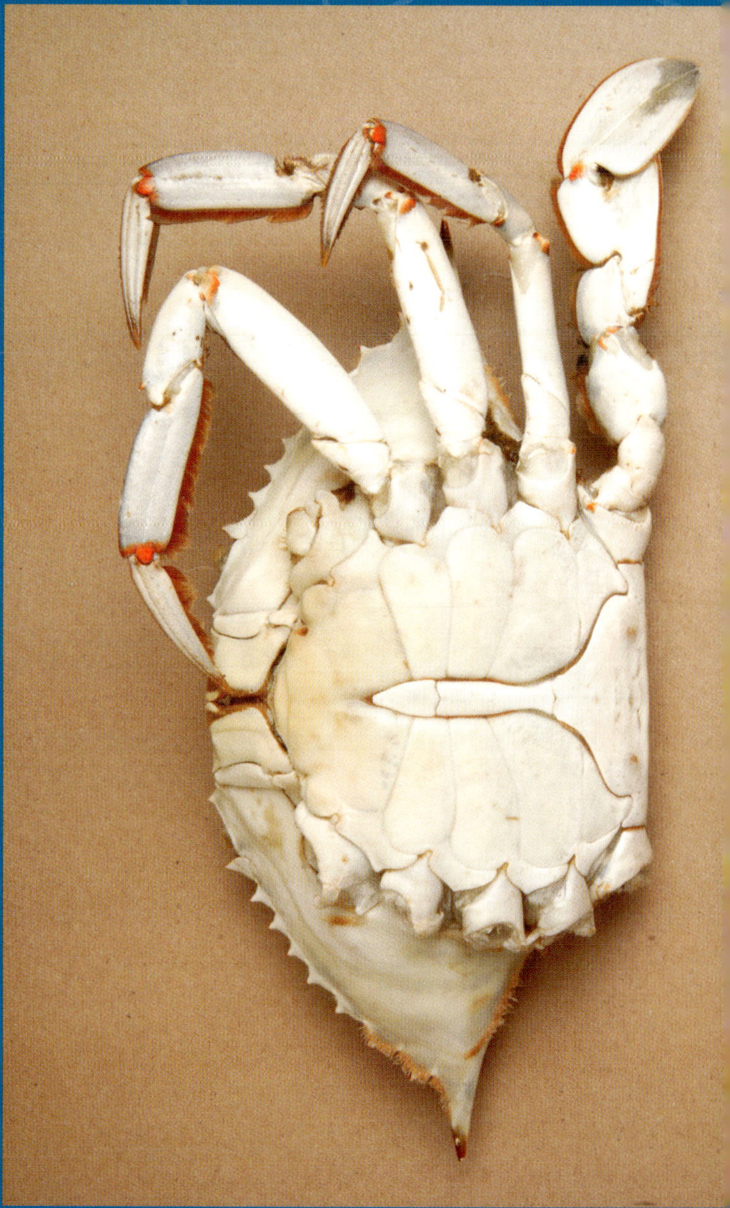

Bottom view of the left walking legs.

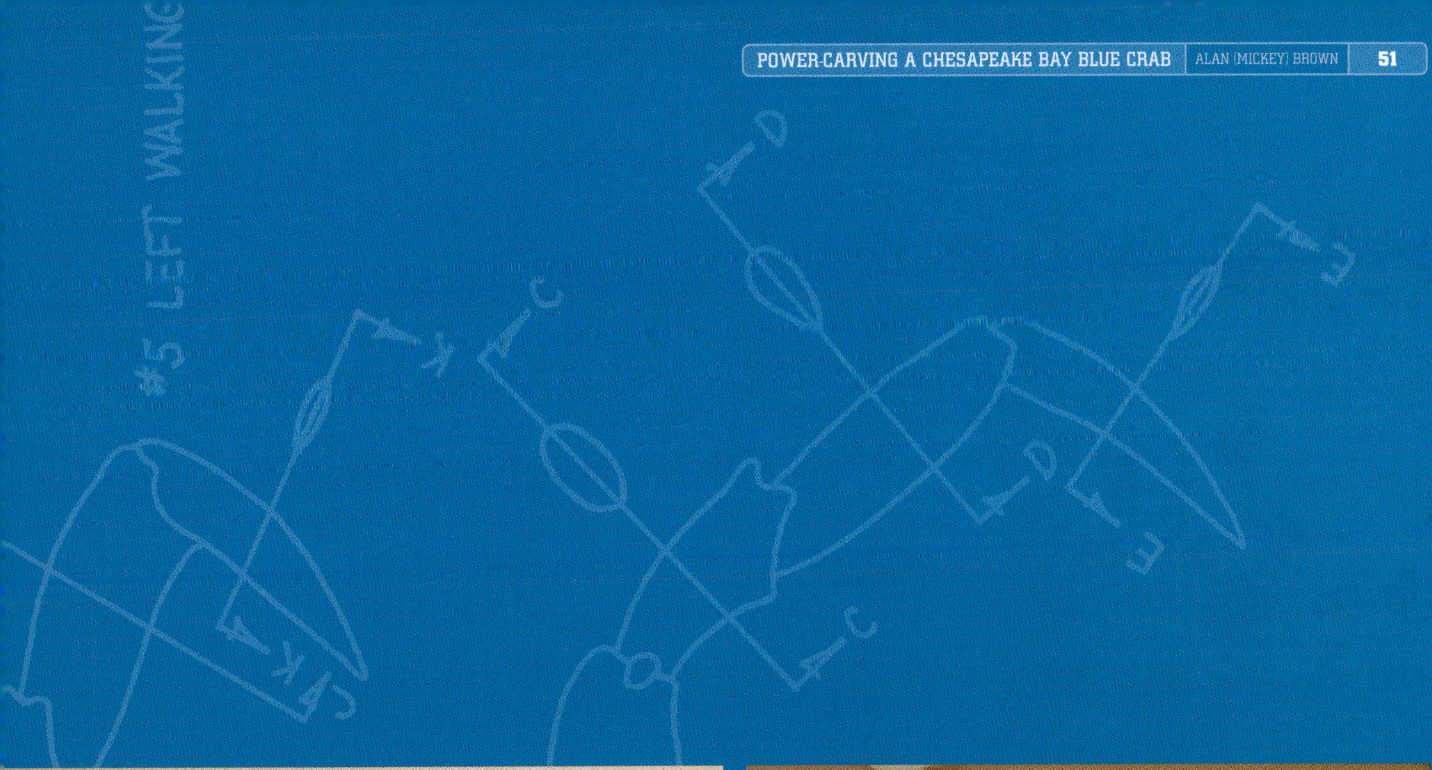

Top view of the left walking legs.

01

After a thorough sanding, paint a coat of Jo Sonja's Gesso as a wood sealer.

02

Sand the sealer coat lightly with 220 grit sandpaper and then apply a coat of Apple Antique White acrylic paint.

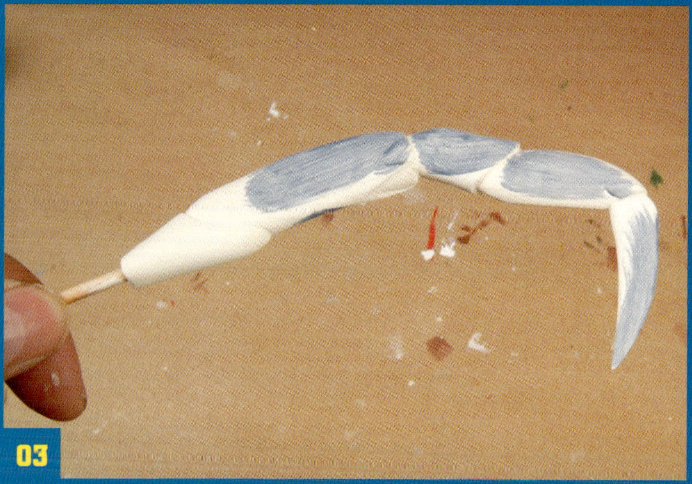

03

Paint a very light, thin coat of Colonial Light Blue on all areas that show a blue tint.

04

Paint a very fine line of Cinnamon Brown into all of the leg joints to identify each moving joint. A pointed 1/8" dowel will apply a finer line than a brush.

05

Paint each raised point a Deep Red Rouge mixed with a touch of Orange.

06

Lightly sand and blend all colors together using a fine 3M pad or 400-grit sandpaper.

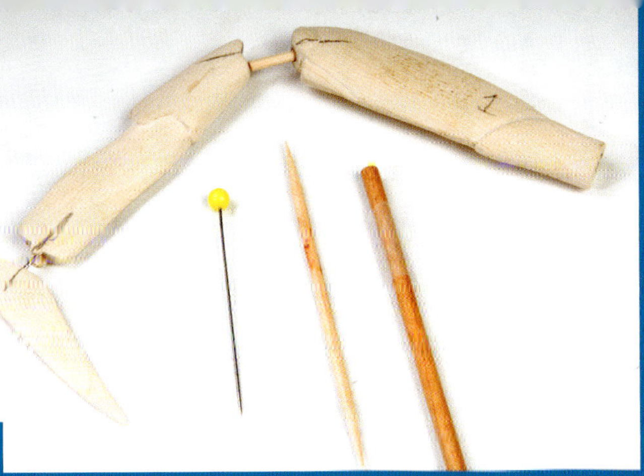

01

Attach parts together in the desired location using cut pins, rounded toothpicks, or a 1/8" dowel rod to add additional support when gluing the parts together.

THE PEREOPODS | 10

After carving the body and the many parts of the walking legs, swimming legs, and claws, it is time to assemble the parts permanently in a realistic and pleasing position. Keep in mind that the crab has great flexibility in every joint of every pereopod. It would be difficult to position any leg or claw in an unnatural location.

However, at this point, it is important that you have in mind how the crab is to be mounted so that you can mount the legs and claws to accommodate your selected mounting. Do not glue end grain to end grain without adding additional support of pins or rods to provide strength in that joint.

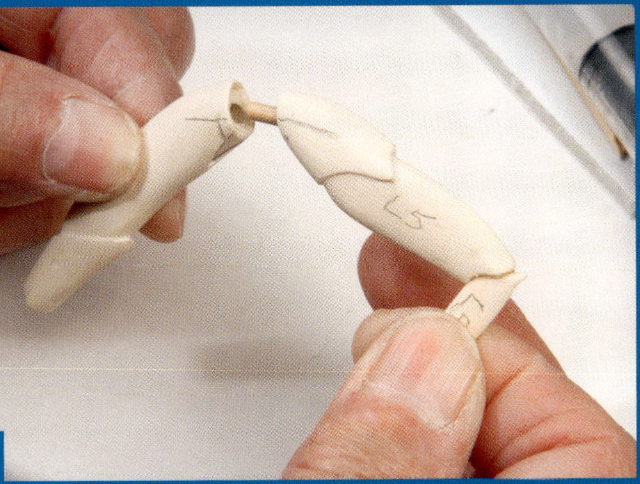

02

Draw a straight line on both joints to help in drilling both pieces so that they form the angle you desire. Select a drill bit slightly larger than the pin to allow some adjustment and ease of gluing. Use a 5-minute epoxy adhesive in gluing the parts together. This will allow you to hold the parts in the desired location until the adhesive hardens. At this time, painting of the individual parts can take place.

03

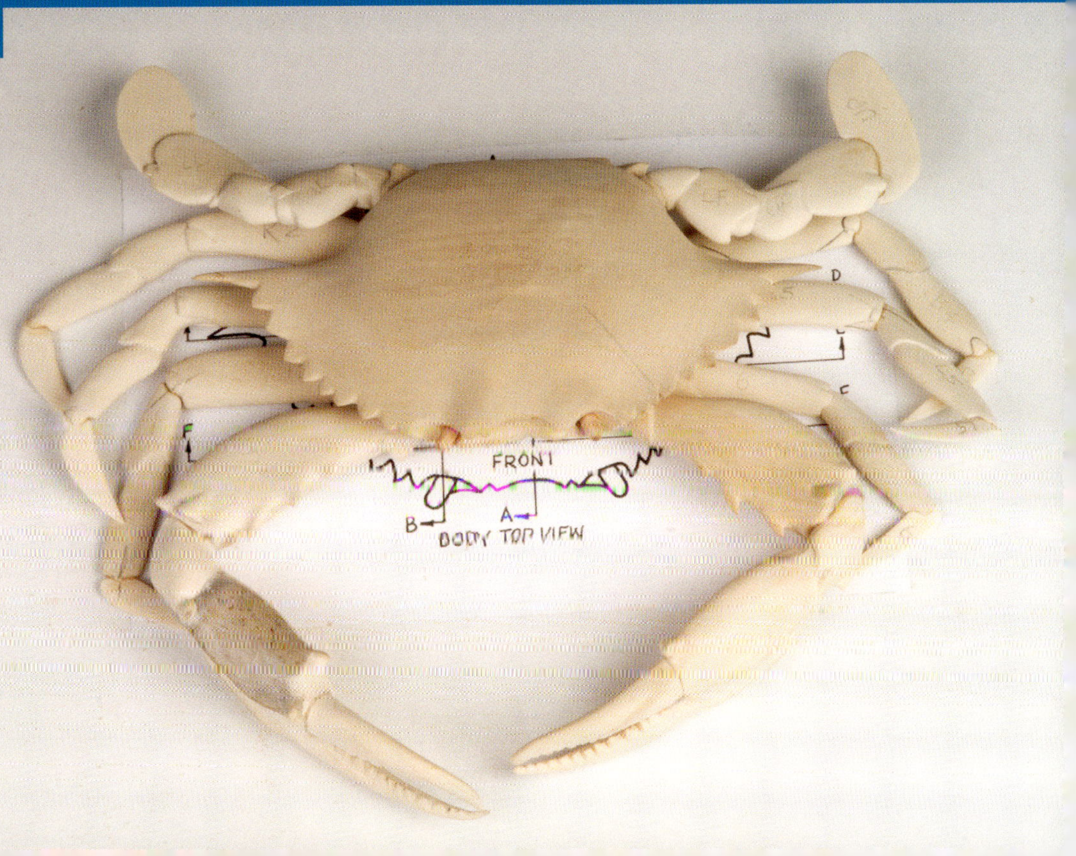

In a similar manner, and only after all painting of the body, legs and claws have been completed, pin and glue the legs and claws to the crab body in the position selected for the mount.

11 | THE BARNACLES & GRASS

When displaying the carved crab, it is essential to display the crab in a natural setting to compliment the crab. An old piece of driftwood that fit the nautical theme was used as a base and only required leveling in three areas to become stable. Determine how the crab will be positioned on the display by holding the crab in various positions. This decision should be made prior to completely assembling the crab so that the claws and walking legs can be positioned to appear as if the crab is climbing the driftwood.

The grasses that were used also offered a nautical background, but had to be carved, shaped, and bent out of very thin tupelo wood. The grasses are painted and then irregularly mounted on the driftwood. To complete the nautical effect, various shapes of barnacles were carved, painted, and mounted randomly to give the appearance of age and salt water on the driftwood.

01

Copy the front and top view of the barnacle on a scrap of tupelo wood, making certain that the wood grain runs vertically. Attach the block to be carved to another scrap block with a wood screw. This will help you hold the small barnacle when carving.

02

Carve the sides of the barnacle into a cone shape and sand all areas.

03

Draw random joints on the barnacle and carve them in with a cylinder carbide cutter. The carved joints should not be very deep.

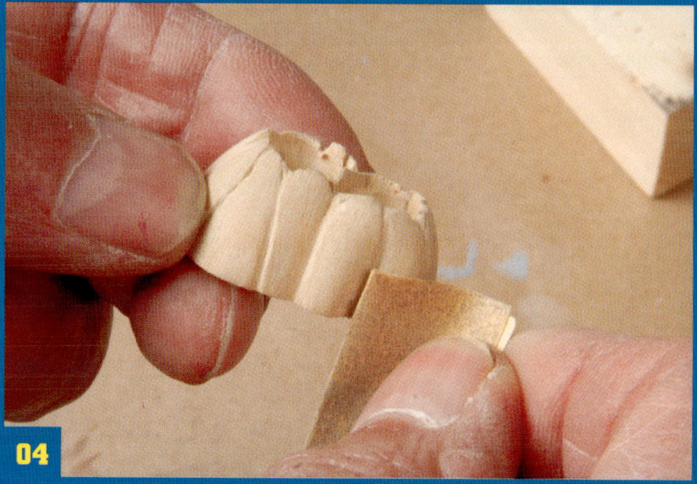

04

Sand all surfaces and joints thoroughly with 220-grit paper.

05

The completed barnacle is first painted with Gesso and then a coat of White paint. Cinnamon Brown can then be applied to the joints and quickly removed to outline the joints.

06

Cut thin tupelo wood strips about 1/16" thick and 1/8" wide. Taper both the width and thickness of the tip of grass to a point with a sharp knife and sand completely with 220 grit sandpaper.

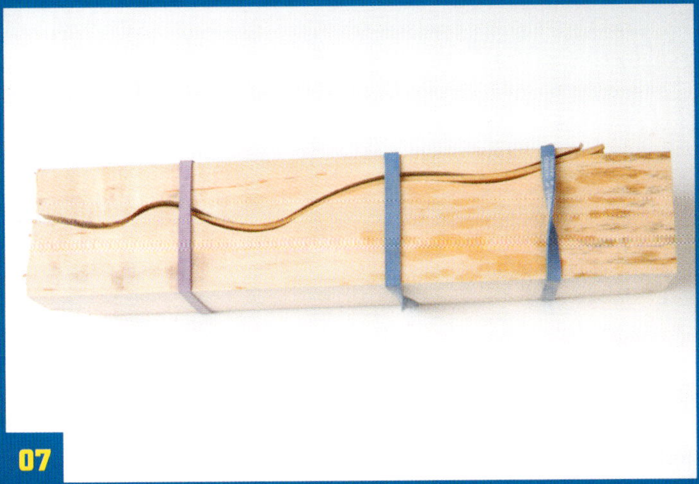

07

From a scrap piece of 2 x 4, cut an irregular curved shaped pattern that will be used to form the shape of the sea grass. Soak the tapered wood strips in water, place them in the 2 x 4 press, and fasten the two halves of the press together with rubber bands until the grass is dry.

08

Paint the grass green leaving some of the tips without paint to simulate a more natural brown dying tip.

09

Mount the grass in the display area by drilling a small hole in the driftwood display. Taper the bottom of the grass and glue one or more of the grass into the drilled hole.

12 | POWER-CARVING A CARICATURE BLUE CRAB

A caricature blue crab carving is one in which certain distinguished features are distorted or exaggerated to produce a comical likeness of a blue crab. The plans shown here exaggerate the claws, eyes, and other features while keeping the number of pereopods and the body shape similar to the true crab. This freedom provides an easy and fun approach to carving as opposed to the detailed carving that is required when trying to duplicate an exact replica of the blue crab.

Caricature carving is not exact and can be very forgiving and enjoyable to the creative carver. While the plans, sectionals, and photographs provide a controlled method of power-carving the crab, feel free to experiment in creating your own caricature crab. The crab can be used as a necklace for a casual appearance at a crab feast or used as a fan or light pull to offer a nautical touch to a room. Inexpensive necklace chains are easily obtained and attached to the hook glued between the exaggerated eyes. If a pull chain is used, simply epoxy the chain into a drilled hole between the eyes. Once carved, the crab can be finished naturally or painted to

represent the colors of a blue crab. On the underside of the crab, the apron is carved to represent either a male or female crab (as illustrated in the caricature plans). The male apron is "T" shaped while the female apron is definitely much wider or pyramid shaped.

The crab is painted in steps similar to the realistic crab without blending and fading the colors together. Apply a base coat of Gesso, followed by the colors you desire. There is much more color freedom allowed in painting a caricature. Finishing the caricature crab can be done in many ways and since we have used tupelo carving wood, which has no attractive grain features, painting is the best solution. If the crab is carved in walnut, oak, or another kind of attractive wood, finish the crab with a clear satin or semi gloss wipe on poly or a spray poly by Minwax.

The caricature crab can also be easily carved in relief (as shown in the redwood covered beam on a crab-eating porch), which offers a nautical atmosphere to the porch setting. Other crab carvings can be found in the *Gallery* section.

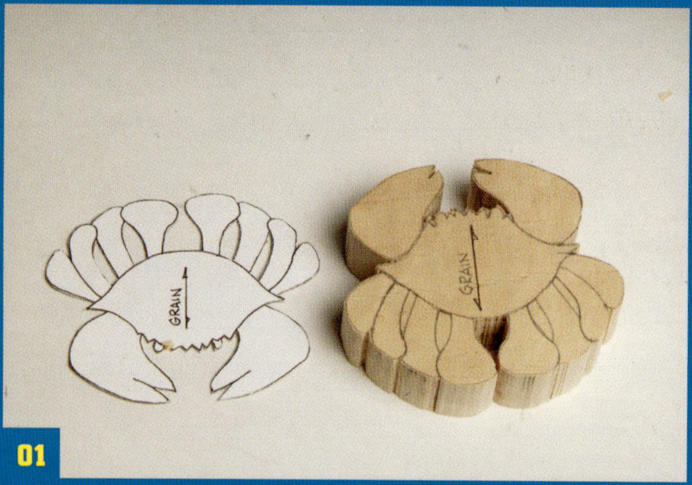

01

Draw the caricature crab on 3/4" thick tupelo wood with the grain vertical as shown and then cut out the crab on the band saw.

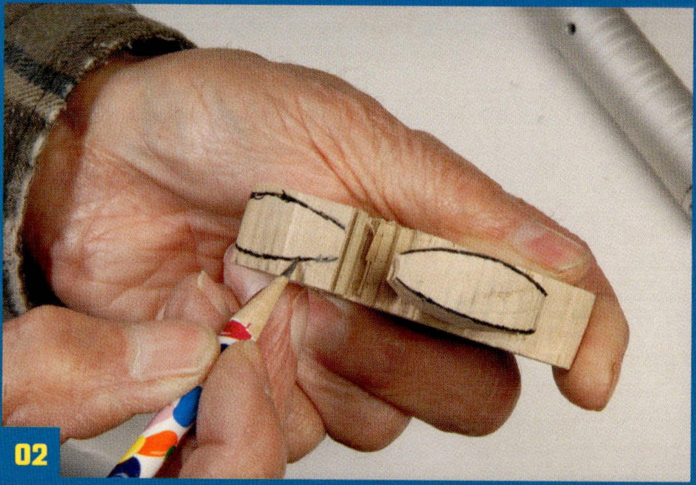

02

Sketch out the thickness of the claws using template BB.

03

Rough out the claw thickness using a cylinder carbide bit.

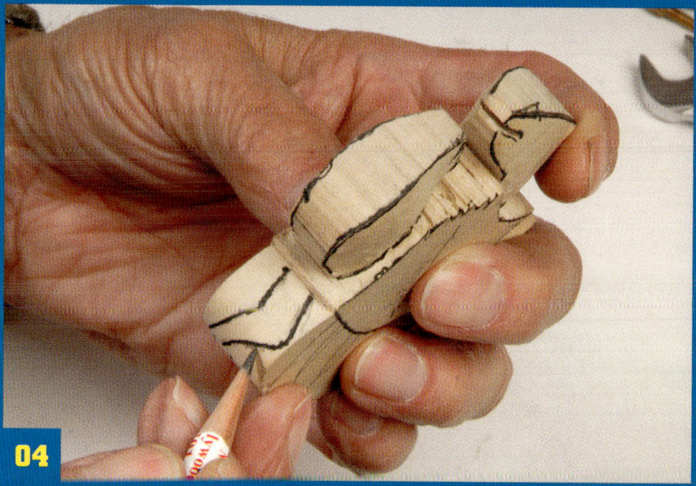

04

Sketch out the complete side view again using template BB.

05

Rough out the thickness of the walking and swimming legs using a ball nose fine Typhoon bit.

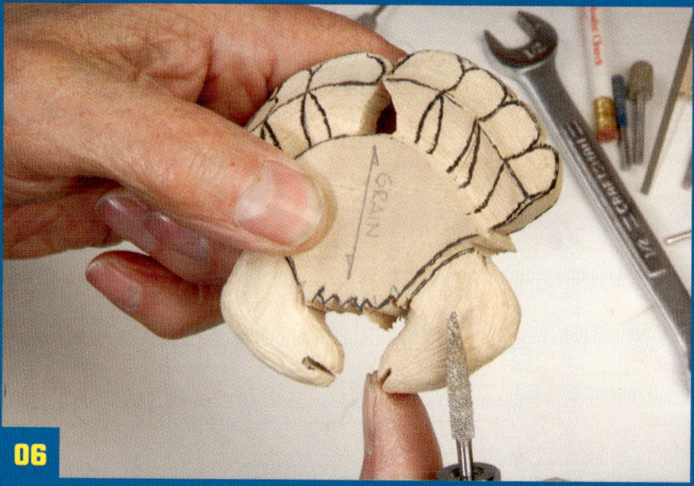

06

Round the claws to an elliptical shape as shown in sectional template BB (refer to Chapter 2).

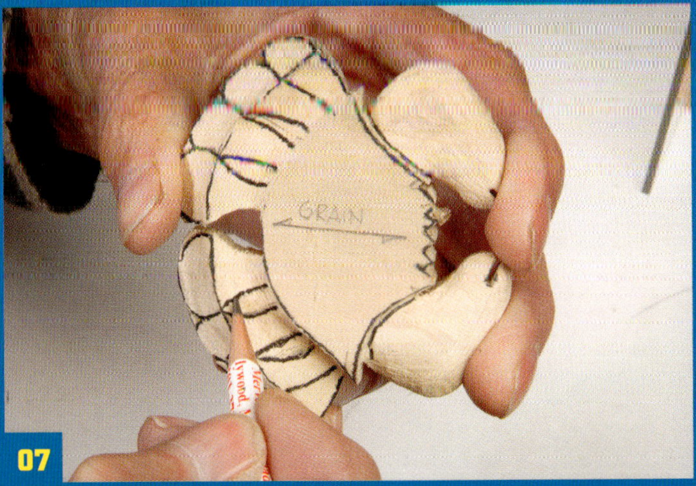

07

Sketch the top view of the eight walking and swimming legs.

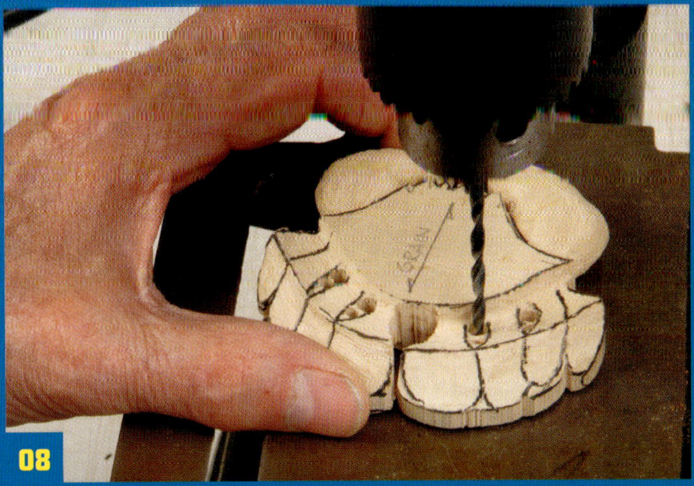

08

Drill a 1/8" hole between the legs and completely through the thickness of the wood.

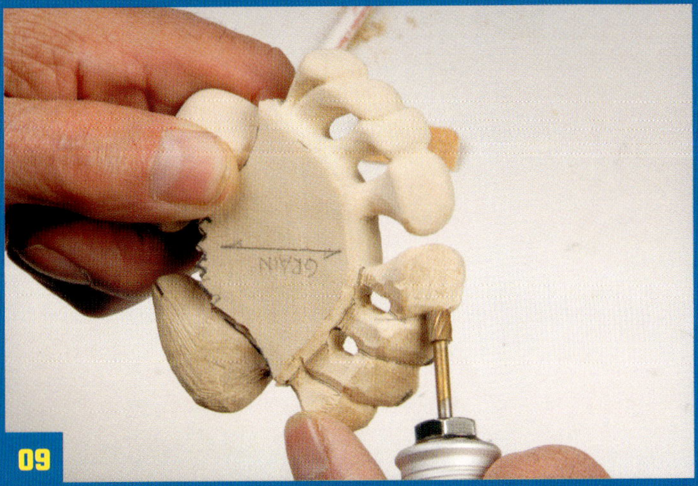

09

Begin rounding all edges of the legs using appropriate shaped bits that are available and will get the job done.

10

Round all edges of the body making a definite line between the legs and pinchers, again using the cylinder carbide bit. Drill 1/8" eye holes making certain that the holes are drilled pointing outward (tip to tip) and slightly up. The drawn pencil lines will assist in aligning the drill bit.

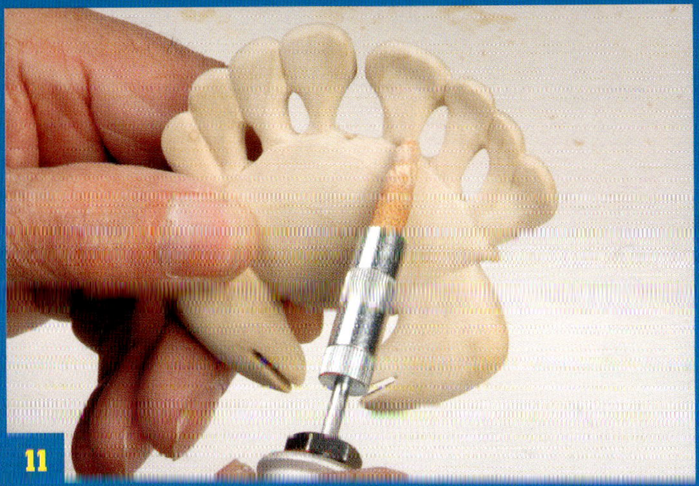

11

Sand the body and the legs using the Marsh sander, Soft drum sander, or 150 grit hand sanding.

12

Glue rounded 1/8" dowels into the eye sockets and allow them to stick out from the body about 1/4".

13

Make a copper eye out of 14-gauge wire, drill a hole below the eyes, and epoxy the copper eye into the drilled hole. A necklace chain has been attached to the copper eye.

14

The top of the Caricature Crab is painted in solid colors of Light Blue, Light Beige, Off-white, and Red. However, any colors can be used on a caricature.

15

The bottom of the crab is painted an Off-white with the crab apron outlined in Brown. The stained crab and ear rings are finished naturally and illustrate a design freedom from the painted crab.

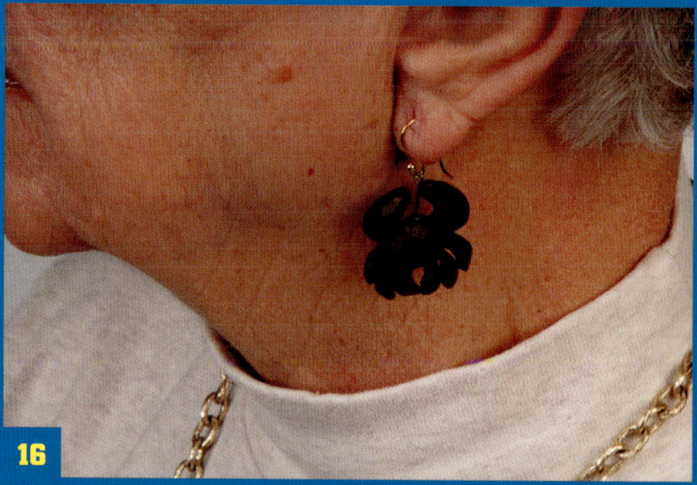

16

By reducing the plans, earrings may be carved in miniature and worn as a matching set.

GALLERY

A relief carving of a blue crab carved in northern white birch with a double oil stain finish.

A blue heron carved in relief on the face of a cedar covered beam. Oil finish.

A crab ceiling fan pull, carved in walnut wood with a natural finish.

A property name carved in relief.

A caricature fish carved in relief.

A large crab hanging from a barnacled rope carved from pine wood and stained red.

Carving of a Blue Heron in characteristic flight with the neck folded in an "S" shape and legs trailing. Carved in tupelo wood with feathers burned in.

An Osprey (Fish Hawk) feeding on a recent fish kill obtained by diving in the water.

Drum Point Lighthouse, Solomons, Maryland.
A relief carving in northern birch with a lightly stained background and a carved rope border.

A Blue Heron carved in relief among grasses and cat tails patiently waiting a seafood meal.